'THE WEE DONEGAL' Revisited

MORE VIEWS OF THE COUNTY DONEGAL RAILWAYS IN COLOUR

ROBERT ROBOTHAM

JOE CURRAN

No 10 railcar is seen at Stranorlar on 22 May 1956. The gentleman holding the papers is railcar motorman Collins Lafferty. The other man is Patsy McArdle, a stores assistant at the important CDR works at Stranorlar. Cans of fuel oil for topping up the tank of the railcar can be seen on the ground next to No 10. The magnificent station stands in the background and an oil tanker is also seen – it carried fuel oil for the railcars from Strabane. A postman waits with his bike on the platform – mails were an important part of the CDR's business. To his right is a CDR lorry that offered both road delivery from stations and direct services and, along with the CDR motor buses, complemented railway operations.

ColourRail

About the Authors

Robert Robotham is a lifelong professional railwayman, having joined British Rail in 1981. His interest in railways was inspired by watching the famous Annesley to Woodford 'Runners' or 'Windcutters' on the Great Central main line near his home city, Nottingham. The author of a number of railway books, with both Ian Allan and Colourpoint, Robert's interest extends to both British and Irish railways – the County Donegal being his favourite.

Robert served with the Territorial Army, in Yeomanry regiments, for 22 years, but has now devoted most of his spare time to his family and friends. He now works for Railtrack Plc, following previous roles with InterCity, Red Star, Freightliner, Railfreight Petroleum and BR Telecomms.

Robert would especially like to thank his friend Joe Curran for all his generous help with both County Donegal books. He would also like to thank Cherri, Jake, Georgie and Bertie for their support whilst writing this book.

Joe Curran is an optometrist (retired) and a Fellow of the College of Optometrists. However, he has been a lifelong railway enthusiast and transport historian and has frequently been on radio. This enthusiasm owes something to the fact that he was a son of BL Curran, the last Manager and Secretary of the County Donegal Railway! He is also a former shareholder in the Strabane and Letterkenny Railway Company. Joe was closely involved with the CDR in its last years and has an unrivalled knowledge of its staff and operating practices.

Two other members of Joe's family were closely involved with transport. His brother Leo Curran, FIMechE, a Chartered Engineer, was initially a junior engineer on the GNR at Dundalk. He then moved to the West Clare section of CIÉ, where he introduced railcars similar to CDR Nos 19 and 20. He later served on British Rail and in South Africa, before joining Harland and Wolff as Director of engine building. Another brother, Raymond, was formerly Road Transport Supervisor of the CDR and was closely involved in the Dr Cox scheme.

All rights reserved. No part of this publication may be reproduced, stored in a retrieval system or transmitted in any form or by any means, electronic, mechanical, photocopying, scanning, recording or otherwise, without the prior written permission of the copyright owners and publisher of this book.

6 5 4 3 2 1

© Robert Robotham and Joe Curran
Newtownards 2002

Designed by Colourpoint Books, Newtownards
Maps drawn by Barry Craig for Colourpoint
Printed by W&G Baird Ltd

ISBN 1 904242 02 2

Colourpoint Books
Unit D5, Ards Business Centre
Jubilee Road
NEWTOWNARDS
County Down
Northern Ireland
BT23 4YH
Tel: 028 91820505
Fax: 028 91821900
E-mail: info@colourpoint.co.uk
Web-site: www.colourpoint.co.uk

Cover Pictures

Front cover
Class 5A No 2 *Blanche* makes a fine sight as she leaves Donegal town for Stranorlar.
P Whitehouse/ColourRail

Back cover
No 19 railcar is seen at Killybegs on 3 August 1959.
ES Russell/ColourRail

No 5 *Drumboe* takes water from the column at Ballyshannon on 4 August 1958. It is pleasant to know that this locomotive is now under restoration at Donegal town.
ES Russell/ColourRail

CONTENTS

Preface 5

Introduction 6

Historical Background 9

Main Photographic Sections

Stations 11

Steam Locomotives 47

Railcars, Trailers and Phoenix 57

Coaching Stock 66

Railcars on Passenger Services 72

Steam Hauled Passenger Services 83

Steam Hauled Freight Services 94

The Bus Replacements 107

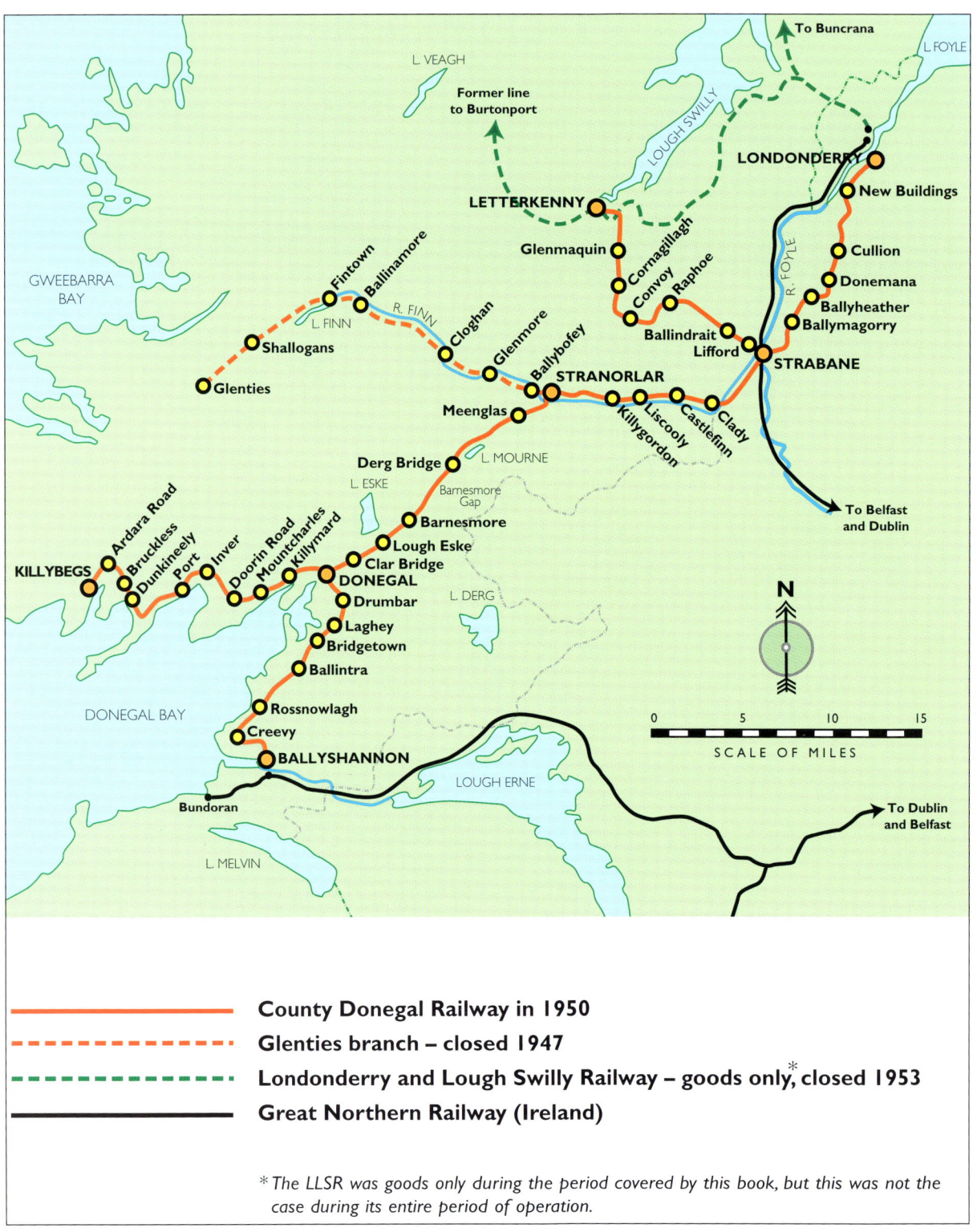

PREFACE

Like all railways of the era, the 'Donegal' did its best to serve its people and develop its services, whilst endeavouring to get a return for its shareholders and directors. Like its fellows, it only had modest financial success at the best of times (war times), whilst undoubtedly fulfilling the need for the transportation of passengers and goods, if not always expeditiously, at least inexpensively.

At the same time, through its social services and devotion of its staff, it forged a loyalty between management, customers and workers which to this day is appreciatively remembered. It opened up the beauty spots and made access possible to thousands who would never have known them.

'To Live in the Hearts of Those We Leave Behind is Not to Die'

Joe Curran, Omagh, July 2002

Looking across Lough Mourne towards the Barnesmore Gap on 22 May 1956. The track of the railway can be seen on the right. Time for the 08.55 railcar from Donegal. *ColourRail*

INTRODUCTION

An article in the May 1969 edition of *Railway Magazine* imparted some information about what it called the 'County Donegal Remains'. It mentioned that locomotives and rolling stock of the County Donegal Railway (CDR) purchased by Dr Ralph Cox, an American, had not been, as hoped, transported to the United States, but were still extant at various locations on the former network of 3'0"gauge lines that had once stretched to 124½ miles. The rail system had closed on the last day of 1959, and at the various auctions that followed closure, some items had been sold to Dr Cox for a planned railway in the USA. However, the cost of shipping them to the USA was in the region of £35,000 and this sum had proved difficult to find. Thus, in 1967, an advert was placed in *The Times*, putting all the purchases up for sale again.

However, there seems to have been no buyer (I should imagine that in 2002 all the items would have gone like the proverbial 'hot cakes') and thus the stock was abandoned to its fate. Class 5 2-6-4 tank locomotives *Meenglas* and *Drumboe* stood at Strabane, where the 'Wee Donegal' (as it was locally known), connected with the now also closed Derry Foyle Road to Dundalk Barrack Street standard gauge line of the former Great Northern. The station site was required for 'development'. Here also were bogie coaches and other items, but the main problem was that the whole site was to be re-developed and it was unclear as to who should pay for the removal of the locomotives and rolling stock.

The County Donegal Railways Joint Committee lived on, wholly a road operator since 1 January 1960, and no longer owned the stock, which was now Dr Cox's property. The other matter was that the ravages of time and vandalism had taken their toll; all the locomotives had their fittings removed, and the coaches, which were wooden, had been stripped of seats and other fittings. Windows were also smashed. Further down the Finn Valley at Stranorlar, the CDRJC's headquarters, it was a similar scene without the vandalism, but at least No 12 railcar and locomotive No 6 *Columbkille* were under cover in the former 'General Store'. No 14 railcar was also stored there, together with a coach.

Dismantled rails that had been moved to the site from other parts of the network, as well as other ferrous items, had all been sold to the Hammond Lane Metal Company of Dublin.

On the Strabane and Letterkenny road, the locomotive that had been used to demolish the line, 'Baltic' tank No 11 *Erne*, had been stored at Letterkenny. Unbelievably, she survived until early 1969 but the steam preservation movement not realising her significance, she was sold for scrap and was broken up – thus the last 3'0" gauge 'Baltic' tank in the British Isles was lost. With her went many wagon frames, as the station site was cleared to make way for more 'development'. At least the main buildings survived as a bus station operated by the CDRJC. At Killybegs it was much the same, the station site purchased by the local Board of Works. Those unlucky items of rolling stock cut off there, including wagons Nos 75 and 84, were dismantled where they stood. A new CDRJC office, it was reported in *Railway Magazine*, was to be built elsewhere.

This was a sad end to what was a great railway system that had served the people of Donegal for 96 years. The railcars and locomotives that had operated the passenger and freight services were used to assist in demolishing the lines, tracks were ripped up and rails were transported to the main stations for the attention of the scrap merchants.

The following pages tell the story of the County Donegal Railways Joint Committee in the last decade of its life as a railway operator. There will be no sign of decline in any of the photographs. The standard of operation, cleanliness and condition of the railcars, locomotives and rolling stock demonstrate this, as do the smartness of the staff.

It was really only the railway's inability to generate sufficient capital to renew its fixed assets, track and structures that finished the CDR's rail operations. A 'reserve' fund that had wisely been kept for this purpose had run out by the late 1950s and it was decided to move to total road operation by the start of 1960. This was relatively easy for the CDR because it already had a large road lorry fleet and was the licensed freight carrier for the area it covered, as was the Lough Swilly Railway to the north, also an exclusively road operation set up following the closure of its rail services some years before the CDR.

What was lost, however, was the operation of those wonderful 11-coach steam excursions that had stormed through the Barnesmore Gap in the Blue Stack Mountains on their way to the sea from Strabane, carrying passengers from further than that. The brilliant Walker Brothers' railcars and their trailers transformed and prolonged the railway's passenger services, pioneering as they did so the operation of diesel railcars in the whole of the British Isles. The marvellous array of bracket signals and tracks, signal cabins, interlocking ground signals and all of what is now called the 'infrastructure' of the railway vanished too – it had been built up over a considerable length of time but was quickly demolished.

A certain way of life went too. The farmer was no longer able to call in at his local CDR station and order a wagon (which would be there next day) to take his cattle to market. The post office in Lifford had to switch to road vehicles, having been served since 1909 by the train. The fishing fleet got more deliveries and collections by road (albeit CDR), and all other general freight went by road, as did the passengers. No longer were those steam-hauled excursions possible.

The CDR was eventually taken over by CIÉ, for the three Joint Committee members (of which more later) from British Rail had been replaced by CIÉ ones. The lorries were repainted from their crimson and crème livery to black (and re-numbered as they got routine service); at least the buses continued in their former livery. Staff were given new CIÉ uniforms and sold, in the main, CIÉ tickets. The new order had arrived.

This book follows on from the first colour volume *The Last Years of 'The Wee Donegal'* published by Colourpoint in 1998. The discovery of more colour photographs and the interest generated by the first book encouraged the production of this second volume, again with significant input from Joe Curran, son of the last Manager and Secretary of the CDR during its rail operations. Joe's contribution has literally brought both books to life as he is able to identify individuals and provide a wealth of information about railway operations and other matters. It is only fitting that his name should appear on the cover as my co-author, as without him the book would only be half of what it is!

The other thanks are due to all the photographers who made trips to the area to take photographs of the railway. Some of these are no longer with us, but some are very much alive – this book is a tribute to all of them. As always, Ron White of *ColourRail* has been a great help and my thanks are due to him for offering most of the following photographs for publication. Indeed, most of these are commercially available as slides from the *ColourRail* catalogue, obtainable from : 5 Treacher's Close, Chesham, Buckinghamshire, HP5 2HD, England.

Lastly, it is important to pay tribute to those who ran the line, in all weathers and at all hours of the day – the railway was truly a 24-hour operation and everyone played their part. Without the cleaner and fire raiser at Strabane there would have been no locomotive to work the train; without the railcar fitter, no service; and without the blacksmiths at Stranorlar, no springs to smooth the ride. There are hundreds more from permanent way ganger right through to the Manager and Secretary himself! Many of these people are seen in the following photographs and identified by Joe Curran.

It is the people that make any railway and their dedication to duty and professionalism shines through in the following pages.

Robert Robotham, Sherborne, July 2002

No 11 Phoenix   **Scale: 4 mm to 1 ft**

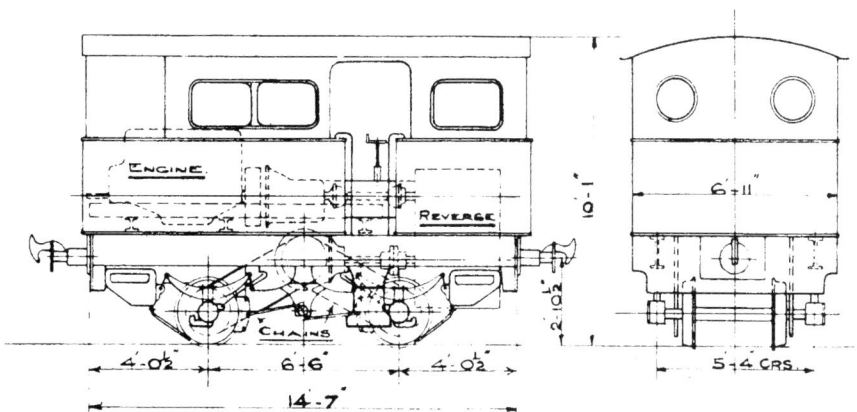

OUTLINE
GENERAL TIME TABLE
(EXCEPT WHERE OTHERWISE STATED THE SERVICES NAMED RUN ON WEEKDAYS)

		a.m.	a.m.	a.m.	a.m.	p.m.	p.m.	p.m.	p.m.	p.m.
LETTERKENNY	dep.	—	8. 0	—	11.15	2.35	5.30	—	6.57	9.30
CONVOY	,,	—	8.31	—	11.45	3. 5	6. 0	—	7.25	10. 0
RAPHOE	,,	—	8.41	—	11.57	3.15	6. 9	—	7.35	10.10
LIFFORD	arr.	—	9. 1	—	12.15	3.35	6.29	—	7.54	10.28
LIFFORD	dep.	—	9. 8	—	12.23	3.46	6.34	—	7.58	10.33
STRABANE	arr.	—	9.10	—	12.25	3.48	6.36	—	8. 0	10.35

		a.m.	a.m.	a.m.	a.m.	p.m.	p.m.	p.m.	p.m.	p.m.
STRABANE	dep.	7.45	9.50	11.20	2.40	4.50	—	6.10	8. 0	
CASTLEFIN	arr.	8. 7	10.12	11.39	2.57	5. 7	—	6.27	8.17	
CASTLEFIN	dep.	8.10	10.20	11.50	3.11	5.12	—	6.30	8.19	
KILLYGORDON	,,	8.19	10.29	12. 0	3.20	5.21	—	6.40	8.28	
STRANORLAR	arr.	8.31	10.40	12.12	3.32	5.33	—	6.50	8.40	

							SA.O.		Sundays only Noon
STRANORLAR	dep.	8.33	—	12.17	3.40	5.55	—	7. 0	—
DONEGAL	arr.	9.24	—	1. 9	4.30	6.44	—	7.51	—

DONEGAL	dep.	9.29	—	1.35	6.10	—	—	—	8. 3	
BALLINTRA	,,	9.50	—	2. 1	6.33	—	—	—	8.24	
ROSSNOWLAGH	,,	10. 1	—	2.11	6.43	—	—	—	8.34	— 12. 0
BAL'YSHAN'ON	arr.	10.19	—	2.25	6.58	—	—	—	8.52	12.20

							SA.O.		
DONEGAL	dep.	9.30	—	1.35	4.55	6.46	—	7.58	
M'TCHARLES	,,	9.45	—	1.46	5.11	7. 1	—	8. 9	
INVER	,,	10. 3	—	2. 3	5.25	7.16	—	8.25	
DUNKINEELY	,,	10.16	—	2.16	5.38	7.29	—	8.37	
KILLYBEGS	arr.	10.35	—	2.35	6. 1	7.50	—	9. 0	

SA.O.— Saturdays Only.

		a.m.	a.m.	a.m.	a.m.	p.m.	p.m.	p.m.	SA.O. p.m.	S.O. a.m.
KILLYBEGS	dep.	—	—	7.45	9.27	—	12.30	3.50	—	6.35
DUNKINEELY	,,	—	—	8. 7	9.48	—	12.50	4.10	—	6.55
INVER	,,	—	—	8.22	10. 1	—	1. 5	4.26	—	7.18
M'TCHARLES	,,	—	—	8.36	10.14	—	1.20	4.40	—	7.32
DONEGAL	arr.	—	—	8.50	10.29	—	1.33	4.55	—	7.46

BAL'YSHA'NON	dep.	—	—	8. 0	—	—	12. 0	4. 0	7.10	—	10.30
ROSSNOWLAGH	,,	—	—	8.18	—	—	12.18	4.18	7.25	—	10.50
BALLINTRA	,,	—	—	8.27	—	—	12.28	4.27	7.34		
DONEGAL	arr.	—	—	8.50	—	—	12.55	4.50	7.58		

| DONEGAL | dep. | — | — | 8.55 | 10.34 | — | 1.42 | 5. 0 | — | 7.58 |
| STRANORLAR | arr. | — | — | 9.49 | 11.24 | — | 2.35 | 5.52 | — | 8.45 |

STRANORLAR	dep.	6.45	8.45	9.55	11.29	1.20	2.40	6. 5		
KILLYGORDON	,,	6.57	8.55	10. 7	11.41	1.32	2.52	6.15		
CASTLEFIN	arr.	7. 7	9. 5	10.15	11.49	1.40	3. 0	6.27		
CASTLEFIN	dep.	7.10	9.10	10.25	11.57	1.45	3. 9	6.32		
STRABANE	arr.	7.28	9.30	10.40	12.12	2. 0	3.25	6.50		

										p.m.
STRABANE	dep.	8.10	—	11.20	—	2.35	5.35	8.10	—	11.55
LIFFORD	arr.	8.12	—	11.22	—	2.37	5.37	8.12	—	11.57
LIFFORD	dep.	8.19	—	11.32	—	2.50	5.45	8.19	—	12.10
RAPHOE	,,	8.40	—	11.54	—	3.14	6.10	8.39	—	12.32
CONVOY	,,	8.48	—	12. 2	—	3.22	6.18	8.47	—	12.40
LETTERKENNY	arr.	9.18	—	12.32	—	3.52	6.47	9.15	—	1.17

S.O.—SUNDAYS ONLY.

ALL SERVICES OPERATED BY RAILCARS WHICH WILL STOP AT STATIONS AND HALTS

Connections to and from Scotland via Belfast and Glasgow direct

(WEEK-DAYS ONLY)

(A thin line / between the hour and minute figures indicates p.m.)

KILLYBEGS	dep.	12/30
INVER	,,	1/ 5
DONEGAL	,,	1/42
*DUNGLOE	,,	12/ 0
*GLENTIES	,,	1/ 0
STRANORLAR	,,	2/40
LETTERKENNY	,,	2/35
BELFAST (Gt. Victoria St.)	arr.	7/ 0
BELFAST (Donegall Quay)	dep.	7/ 0 to 8/45
GLASGOW (Lancefield Quay)	arr.	8. 0 to 9. 0

GLASGOW (Lancefield Quay)	dep.	7/ 0 to 8/45
BELFAST (Donegall Quay)	arr.	7. 0
BELFAST (Gt. Victoria St.)	dep.	8.25
LETTERKENNY	arr.	12/32
STRANORLAR	,,	12/12
*GLENTIES	,,	1/40
*DUNGLOE	,,	6/ 5
DONEGAL	,,	1/ 9
INVER	,,	2/ 3
KILLYBEGS	,,	2/35

* — Omnibus connections to and from Stranorlar.

Connections to and from Scotland via Londonderry and Glasgow direct

(WEEK-DAYS)

(A thin line / between the hour and minute figures indicates p.m.)

KILLYBEGS	dep.	12/30
INVER	,,	1/ 5
DONEGAL	,,	1/42
*DUNGLOE	,,	12/ 0
*GLENTIES	,,	1/ 0
STRANORLAR	,,	2/40
LETTERKENNY	,,	2/35
LONDONDERRY (Foyle St.)	arr.	5/ 5
LONDONDERRY (Princes Quay)	dep. (A)	7/ 0
GLASGOW (Broomielaw)	arr.	7. 0 to 8. 0

GLASGOW (Broomielaw)	dep. (B)	6/ 0
LONDONDERRY (Princes Quay)	arr.	6. 0 to 7. 0
LONDONDERRY (Foyle St.)	dep.	6.55
LETTERKENNY	arr.	9.18
STRANORLAR	,,	8.31
*GLENTIES	,,	10.10
*DUNGLOE	,,	11/ 5
DONEGAL	,,	9.24
INVER	,,	9.58
KILLYBEGS	,,	10.35

* — Omnibus connections to and from Stranorlar.
A — Tuesdays, Thursdays and Saturdays.
B — Mondays, Wednesdays and Fridays.

HISTORICAL BACKGROUND

The railways that eventually formed the County Donegal network came into being from 7 September 1863. A standard gauge line, running from Strabane to Stranorlar along the Finn Valley, had finally been opened after the usual trouble of getting the funding to match the amount of work required. Inspired by Lord Lifford and Sir Samuel Hayes, two local landowners, the Finn Valley Railway connected at Strabane to the Irish North Western (INWR) line to Derry. The Finn Valley shared Strabane station and the INWR provided the locomotives and rolling stock for the line under contract to the Finn Valley – for which they were paid 35% of receipts and £385 per annum for the use of Strabane station.

The railway did not do well. There were complaints from the Finn Valley board to the INWR about operating inefficiencies and it was believed that the annual rental price was too high. With no resolution in sight, the Finn Valley considered various options, including building their own station at Strabane, but in the end opted to buy their own rolling stock and continue using the existing station. The new arrangements came into effect on the 1 November 1872. All the Irish North Western were contracted to do was provide the locomotives – all operations, coaching stock and staff were provided by the Finn Valley itself.

Lord Lifford then pioneered a new route – this time a narrow gauge line through to Donegal town from Stranorlar – under a separate company called the West Donegal. This line passed through the Blue Stack Mountains and the famous Barnesmore Gap. Lack of funding saw the route finish four miles away from Donegal town at Druminin, but services, operated by the Finn Valley, started on 25 April 1882. A dual gauge interchange station was built at Stranorlar. But due to the lack of a station in Donegal (a horse-drawn road coach service was provided as a connection) the line was not a success and by 1886 more money was raised to get it into Donegal, where it leased the station from a separate company for £200 per annum.

One of the three great managers that the railway was privileged to have had become company Secretary in August 1890. RH Livesey came from the North Wales Narrow Gauge Railway and recommended that the Finn Valley line convert to 3'0" gauge; a considerable saving in costs was expected and gone would be the arrangement with the former INWR (now part of the Great Northern) to provide standard gauge locomotives. The change to narrow gauge was carried out over one weekend, 13 to 15 July 1894. Also, a new bridge was constructed over the River Mourne at Strabane.

Additional routes were added, at a cost of £126,886, mainly funded by the Light Railways (Ireland) Act, the government being keen to stop the local population moving out of Ireland following the Famine. This Act funded extensions to Killybegs from Donegal, opening in 1893, and from Stranorlar to Fintown and Glenties, opening in 1895. Further lines were added, with the important link to Derry allowing the railway to reach its main source of import traffic without having to rely on the Great Northern, and a branch from Donegal town to Ballyshannon was opened in 1905. The Donegal Railway – as it was named from 1892 on amalgamation of the West Donegal and the Finn Valley – was now 105 miles in total.

As traffic, both freight and passenger, grew, new more powerful locomotives of 4-4-4T, 4-6-4T and 2-6-4T wheel arrangement were introduced to replace the originals. These were all impressive machines and with them came more wagons and coaches. Many of these can be seen in the 1950s photographs which follow. When Livesey retired, his son, 'Young Livesey' as he was known, but more formally RM Livesey, joined the board as Traffic Superintendent.

On 1 May 1906 came another major change. The Belfast and Northern Counties Railway had been purchased by the Midland Railway of England in 1903 and they ran this line through the Northern Counties Committee (NCC). The Midland then tried to buy the Donegal Railway, to which the Great Northern objected. It was then proposed that the Midland and the Great Northern should purchase the Donegal Railway, and this they did on 1 May 1906. Three members from each owning company were placed on the committee which covered all routes, with the exception of the Derry to Strabane line which was wholly owned by the Midland but operated by the new County Donegal Railways Joint Committee, the name of the new company.

It was under their management that the last piece of the network jigsaw was put into place, with the Strabane to Letterkenny road opening on 1 January 1909, a brave challenge to the Londonderry and Lough Swilly 3'0" gauge system to the north.

The history of the 'Wee Donegal', as it was locally known, was then dominated by two men who were instrumental in modernising it and running the operation in such a way that kept it open for rail services until the last day of 1959, when most other Irish narrow gauge lines had closed (only The West Clare surviving the CDR).

The first of these men was Henry Forbes who became Secretary of the CDRJC lines in 1910. He was from the Great Northern and progressed, after holding the post of Traffic Manager, to Manager and Secretary in 1928. Forbes was a moderniser and he saw the railway through the difficult time of the partition of Ireland into the Irish Free State and Northern Ireland.

This meant that the railway now crossed an international border in two places, Lifford on the Letterkenny road and on the Finn Valley at Urney Bridge near Castlefinn.

In these post-World War One years, road transport was developing into a serious threat and Forbes made the decision to cut costs on passenger services by means of railcars. Later, having already purchased four buses to provide connecting services to the trains, Forbes converted two of these into railcars (Nos 9 and the first 10) to supplement the other railcars that were now, in the main, running the passenger timetable.

The railcars were of even greater value as they could also pull a few wagons that contained the important mails traffic, shunt them and pull passenger trailers, thus cheaply increasing capacity. They could also stop virtually anywhere and thus allowed easy patronage, almost like a bus, with many halts opened under Forbes' direction. Crucially these trains did not wear the track out as quickly as steam trains – had Forbes not implemented railcars en masse then there is little doubt that these fixed assets would have needed replacing much earlier and services would have had to have been turned over to road much sooner than they were.

Forbes also realised the importance of freight traffic, with the facilities at Donegal and Glenties being modernised. Motive power was upgraded with the introduction of more locomotives – the Class 5As – thus some of the smaller, out of date, ones could be withdrawn.

Forbes died suddenly in 1943 to be replaced by the CDRJC's Accountant, Bernard Curran, a Northern Counties (NCC) man. This was in the middle of World War Two and at the time much needed to be done to renew the wagon fleet, some of which was getting old. Many wagons were rebuilt, the majority of these having corrugated iron roofs, evident on many of the photographs which follow. Furthermore, and very importantly, much of the permanent way was re-laid at this time.

During World War Two, as with World War One, a guaranteed level of income was promised to the railway which allowed a contingency fund to be built up, reaching £34,150 by the end of the conflict. Curran continued Forbes' policy of integration with buses and it was during his custody that the road freight fleet was built up. Thus the CDR was able to offer door to door road services as well as providing road deliveries from goods trains from the main stations.

This trend was illustrated when the Glenties to Stranorlar line was closed to regular services in December 1947, although it hung on for special workings until 1949, officially closing in 1952. GNR buses, contracted to the CDR, replaced the trains. Next to close was the Strabane to Derry road, in December 1954, traffic passing to road services or the GNR standard gauge line to Derry Foyle Road. This left a fairly modern railcar fleet operating a regular passenger service, with steam hauling the main freight services.

The nationalisation of the 'Big Four' railways in Britain saw the LMS become part of British Railways and thus they came to be represented on the Joint Committee. The GNR had also came under the joint control of both Irish governments from 1953, and a stringent review of operating costs versus income was undertaken. With no level of support from the Joint Committee and with the contingency fund having declined to just over £1,000 by 1958, there was only one option left as the railway could not afford to renew its fixed assets. In May 1959 an application was made to government to replace the Joint Committee's rail services with road ones, still operated by them. Permission was granted and from 1 January 1960 the CDRJC became solely a road operation.

STATIONS

LONDONDERRY VICTORIA ROAD

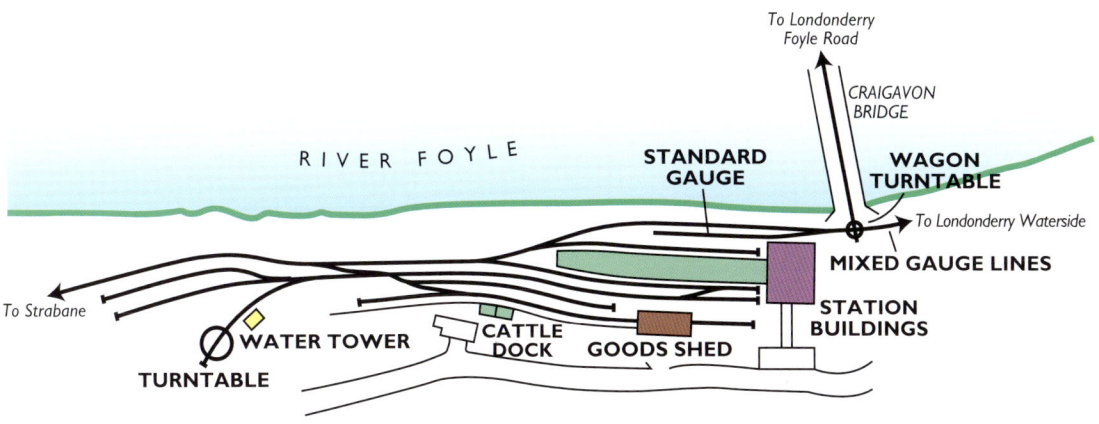

The CDRJC terminus station in Derry was at Victoria Road and a train comprising Class 5A No 1 *Alice* and two coaches is seen here in August 1953, waiting to leave for Strabane. Considerable freight traffic was originally forwarded from here; in addition to coal and other merchandise, there was oil traffic for the fishing fleet at Killybegs, as well as fuel oil for the CDR's railcars. The tanker wagon awaits its next turn of duty on this traffic. In the background the Craigavon Bridge can be seen, a two-tier structure on which the bottom level carried the Londonderry Port and Harbour Commissioners line – originally 5'3" but mixed with 3'0" gauge from 1885.

The network linked the east and west banks of Derry together and totalled approximately six miles. Wagons crossed the Craigavon Bridge by using winches and small turntables but no locomotives were allowed to cross, these only working on the west side. The network linked the Londonderry and Lough Swilly Railway at Graving dock to the GNR line terminus at Foyle Road; over the bridge it linked these two networks to the NCC terminus at Waterside and the County Donegal at Victoria Road.

R Oakley/ColourRail

LONDONDERRY'S RAILWAYS

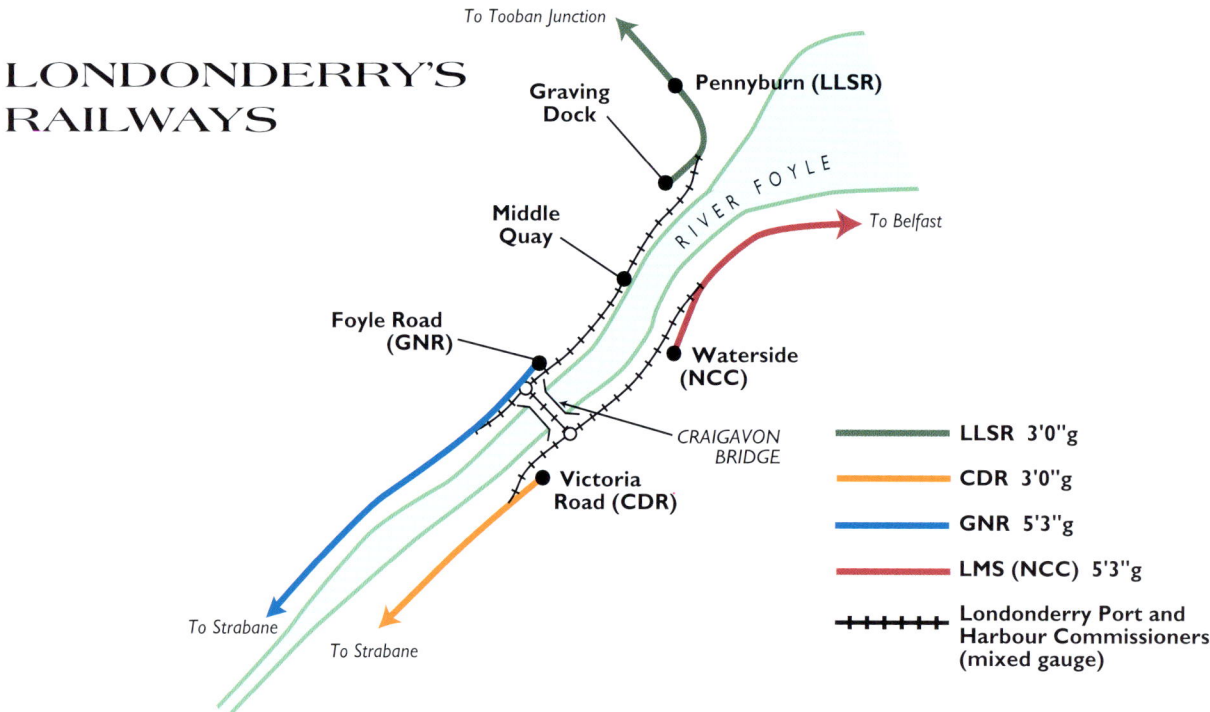

No 1 *Alice* is seen by the loading dock at Victoria Road in November 1953 having just deposited two wagons for unloading. At this time the Strabane to Derry line was owned by the UTA and the operation was subcontracted to the CDRJC, as it had been in Midland and LMS days. Three round trips per day were paid for and the company used the more expensive steam locomotives on the run rather that the cheaper railcars which were better employed on their own services! These trains would also convey wagons of locomotive coal and oil for the railcars from Derry to Strabane. When the Derry line closed, passengers could still travel to the CDR at Strabane on the GNR trains from Foyle Road. Also the CDR had an expanding road fleet and much of the freight traffic was transferred to it, thus keeping it within the company. The total length of this line was 14½ miles from Strabane and it was officially closed on 1 January 1955. Victoria Road itself runs right through to Strabane in postal code terms, surely one of the longest in the British Isles!

WE Robertson/ColourRail

No 12 railcar and Class 5 loco No 6 *Columbkille* are seen near Strabane goods trans-shipment shed in July 1954. The County Donegal wagons are on the left of the shed; the Great Northern wagons are behind the crane on standard gauge tracks. At one stage there were as many as 40 men employed here shovelling turf, etc, from one side to the other – what was known as the 'Tonnage Gang'. Three very typical CDR wagons are in the foreground and the centre one is probably a cattle wagon. The shed to the left of the picture is the engine and railcar shed, which could accommodate two railcars. There was a cleaner operating here at nights who cleaned the locomotives and raised the fires for the day's work ahead. In Joe Curran's time the cleaner/fire raiser was Paddy Floyd. In the foreground are two sets of hand points, one to let the locomotive into the trans-ship siding and the other to let it up into the shunting yard. The railcar and trailer will be forming a service to Stranorlar and then on to Killybegs.

AD Hutchinson/ColourRail

A wider view of the trans-ship shed is seen in this photograph taken on 14 May 1959 as Class 5 No 5 *Drumboe* sets back on a number of wagons at Strabane. The shunter, with pole, can be seen ready to assist with the coupling. The driver is Francie McMenamin, who together with his brother Jim formed a long-standing CDR locomotive crew. The coaches include a passenger van for the guard – no actual brake vans were needed on the CDR as all trains were through piped. This meant that freights always ran with a bogie coach brake van known as a passenger van. The small ground signal was controlled from the CDR signal box and thus prevented access to the main line from the sidings. In order to get out, the locomotive had to whistle the correct code – in this case one 'crow'.

ColourRail

No 20 railcar is seen at Strabane on 2 August 1958 with the 8.10 pm to Letterkenny. Still 'alive' with its sister car No 19 in the Isle of Man, No 20 was always considered to be more powerful than 19. The fence to the right was there as a barrier to allow customs to check passengers and luggage from Letterkenny as they entered Northern Ireland from the Republic of Ireland. In the distance the splash of red and cream is no less than the tractor *Phoenix*, which was shunting the sidings near the trans-shipment shed.

ES Russell/ColourRail

The tractor No 11 *Phoenix* is seen standing on the centre road whilst shunting at Strabane on 18 May 1959. The red wagon is No 14 and being lighter weight than the grey ones was primarily for use with railcars. The grey one is No 257, built in a batch numbered 255 to 284 for the Strabane and Letterkenny railway in 1908. The famous sign now resides in the museum at Cultra and lists all the CDR destinations, including the bus to Glenties (this line having closed from Stranorlar in 1947) and the bus to Creeslough, Gweedore and Burtonport from Letterkenny, destinations once served by the Lough Swilly Railway. The customs man is George Maneely, known as 'Wee George', who is awaiting a train from Stranorlar. This platform was also divided by a barrier fence, and passengers would be checked through and their cases inspected on trestle tables.

JG Dewing/ColourRail

A view from the GN platforms at Strabane as seen in November 1953. A mixed train has arrived into the CDR platform; the two coaches will be removed and then the wagons shunted to the trans-shipment shed. *Phoenix* can just be seen in the background, and will most likely assist with this. On the GN side the north cabin can be seen to the right and behind it is an embankment and over bridge which is the CDR road to Derry. The GN signal in the foreground has a small shunting arm attached to it at ground level and the white disc signals behind it are CDR ones. Over to the left, the double arm signal on the CDR side can be seen, the top arm controlling the Derry road, the bottom controlling the yard access.

ColourRail

No 16 railcar and GNR 4-4-0 No 12 are seen at Strabane on 31 May 1957. On the CDR platform a trestle table can just be seen behind the customs fence – these tables being used to support the cases and luggage during customs examinations. The railcar is backing down next to a GNR M2 bogie van (or vice versa!) after having come in from Stranorlar. Mails were a large source of income for the CDR and it is likely that the mails off the CDR service are to be trans-shipped over to the GN train. *Phoenix* is once more in the background and above the trains is the overhead bridge that blew down in a hurricane in 1961. The nearest grey wagon to the photographer is a cattle wagon, another important source of income for the railway.

FW Shuttleworth/ColourRail

Class 5 2-6-4 tank, No 4 *Meenglas* is seen at Strabane on 16 May 1959 shunting a red wagon – and no doubt there are others attached to this not in the photograph. The train behind is a GNR railcar service coupled to a Y van and a clerestory M1 brake van. No 4 has survived and now resides at the Foyle Valley Railway in Derry, but the future of this railway is currently in doubt.

AG Cramp/ColourRail

Class 5 2-6-4 tank No 6 *Columbkille* and Class 5A 2-6-4 tank No 1 *Alice* are seen at Strabane in July 1954. We have a good view of the customs fence where passengers were checked, the wagons being inspected in the trans-shipment shed as they were sealed in the Strabane direction at Castlefinn. Over to the right a GN locomotive can be seen, probably employed on shunting duties, as Strabane was a very busy yard with over 200 tons of coal a fortnight coming in for the gas works. It is nice to know that locomotive No 6 is now being restored in Derry, but unfortunately No 1 was sold for scrap at auction on 1 March 1961.

AD Hutchinson/ColourRail

No 4 *Meenglas* and No 6 *Columbkille* are seen at Strabane on 22 June 1959. No 4 has a train made up and ready to go up the Finn Valley to Stranorlar, a trip that was easily within the capabilities of the locomotive. It looks as though No 6 will be taking a similar service to Letterkenny. Note the passenger van behind the locomotive. A GN S2 class locomotive can also be seen in the background and a line of red wagons for the railcars stand on the right.

ColourRail

No 12 railcar is seen at Strabane with a Letterkenny service, possibly in June 1953. She is possibly due to pick up a cattle wagon which may be delivered to a station on the Letterkenny road for future shipment of livestock to market. The shunter is Jimmy 'Shunty' Doherty. A fine poster advertises Paddy Whisky and another smaller one Dobbin's Ice Cream. The ubiquitous customs fence and table are also present. The office windows (with bars) can be seen next to the railcar; the nearest window is the booking office. The refreshment rooms were further up the Letterkenny platform.

JM Jarvis/ColourRail

17

The superb lines of 2-6-4 tank No 4 *Meenglas* are well shown as she stands adjacent to the signal cabin and wagon turntable at Strabane. The cleaner has done his job well and the Nasmyth, Wilson builder's plate is well polished. Also the re-railing jack can be seen on the running plate. The mixed gauge of the wagon turntable is well illustrated. It was from here that No 1 railcar left the railway for the Transport Museum in Belfast. A signal on the Letterkenny road can be seen to the left of the locomotive. The Stranorlar line water column can be seen between the chimney and dome of the locomotive.

DWK Jones/ColourRail

No 4 *Meenglas* is seen alongside the loco coal at Strabane on 22 June 1959, prior to working the freight service up the Finn Valley, as seen in the top photograph on page 17. An unusually long line of red railcar wagons can be seen in the background. The weights for the 'throw' points can be clearly seen, painted white. The shed to the right is the Ulster Transport bus depot.

ColourRail

Above: No 5 *Drumboe* stands at Strabane on 15 May 1959. Next to the locomotive are 'empties' (this time bottles, not wagons!) waiting to be returned for filling. These were for Iriscot Ltd of Derry and Curran Brothers of Strabane, one of the latter being the co-author of this book and son of the famous BL Curran, the CDR Manager and Secretary from 1943 to 1966.

C Gammell/ColourRail

Below: No 11, *Erne*, a Class 4, 4-6-4 'Baltic' tank locomotive, and by this stage the only survivor of four sisters, is seen running back into Strabane from the Letterkenny line in March 1958. The locomotive has most likely been shunting and was about to set back onto the line of wagons just visible between the chimney and dome.

WP de Beer/ColourRail

Right: The approach to Strabane was made by crossing the River Mourne and this is well illustrated in this photograph of the bridge. The GN line can be seen on the left. A lamp boy was employed at Strabane station to clean the glasses and put oil in the lamps of the rather fine CDR signals, a good view being had from this one, the outer home signal on the Finn Valley road. It looks as though someone is actually taking his dog for a walk over the bridge, something that would be frowned upon by the authorities. The distant signal can be seen further along the line, as can the GN signal on the approach. The Finn Valley route from Strabane as far as Stranorlar was standard gauge until 16 July 1894 (the conversion being done from 13 to 15 July 1894) and previously joined the GN at Finn Valley Junction approximately where the CDR distant signal is in the photograph. Thus a new bridge was required and hence this new narrow gauge one was constructed.

K Bannister/ColourRail

19

STRABANE

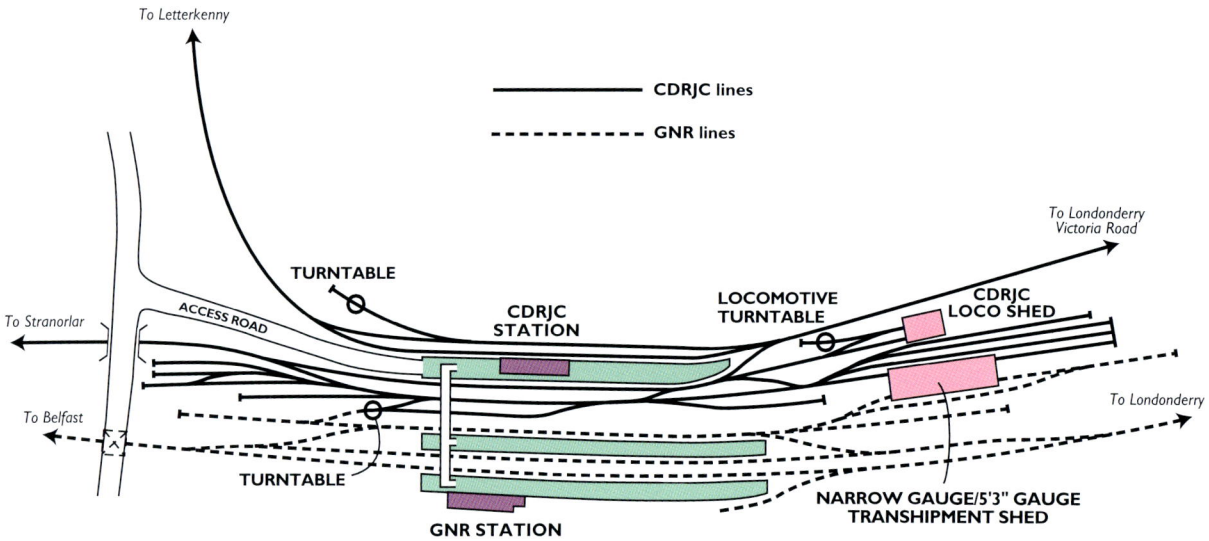

LIFFORD

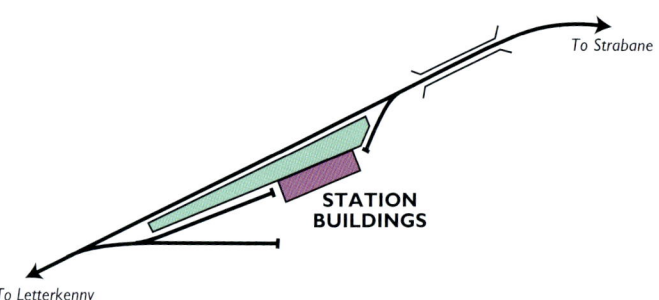

RAPHOE

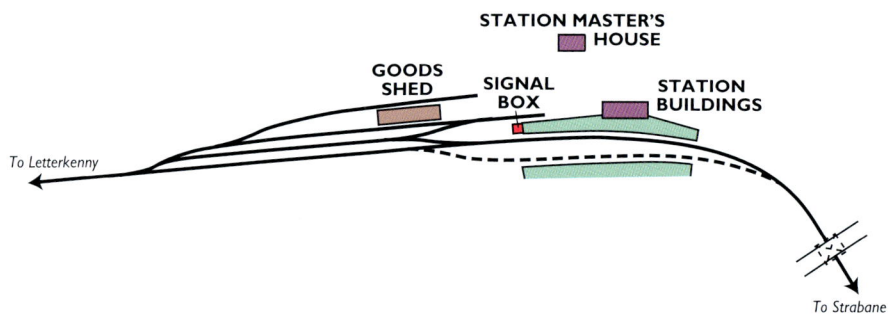

No 2 *Blanche* is seen at Lifford on 20 August 1958. Although a small station, the amount of work that was done there was significant. The CDR station was a major postal station for Donegal and the sorting office was owned by the CDR, built by them and hired to the Post Office. The back door was on the platform and the wagons of mail could be loaded and unloaded by sliding the bags across the platform. It operated nearly 24 hours a day, mails being delivered there up to 1.00 am. Situated on the border, Lifford was a customs post and there were sidings here for wagons to be checked. These were often shunted to and from Strabane – a task usually handled by a steam locomotive or the tractor, *Phoenix*. The fireman is Willie McFeely.

ColourRail

No 18 railcar is seen at Raphoe on 11 May 1958. Raphoe could be classed a major station because it was an important crossing point. No 18 was rebuilt by the GN at Dundalk, following an earlier fire, but this gave it a different appearance – with smaller front windows. However, it was very powerful and second choice as far as Joe Curran is concerned – to No 20. The station at Raphoe is still extant, together with the goods store. In 1958 there was no longer a passing loop and only one platform – the remains of the other are in the foreground. So the down railcar (19 or 20), in the background, from Strabane has already dropped off and picked up its passengers and mails and recessed into the siding, to wait for the Letterkenny to Strabane train to pass, and then proceed. No 18 railcar, having to make important connections at Strabane, has been given priority.

JG Dewing/ColourRail

LETTERKENNY

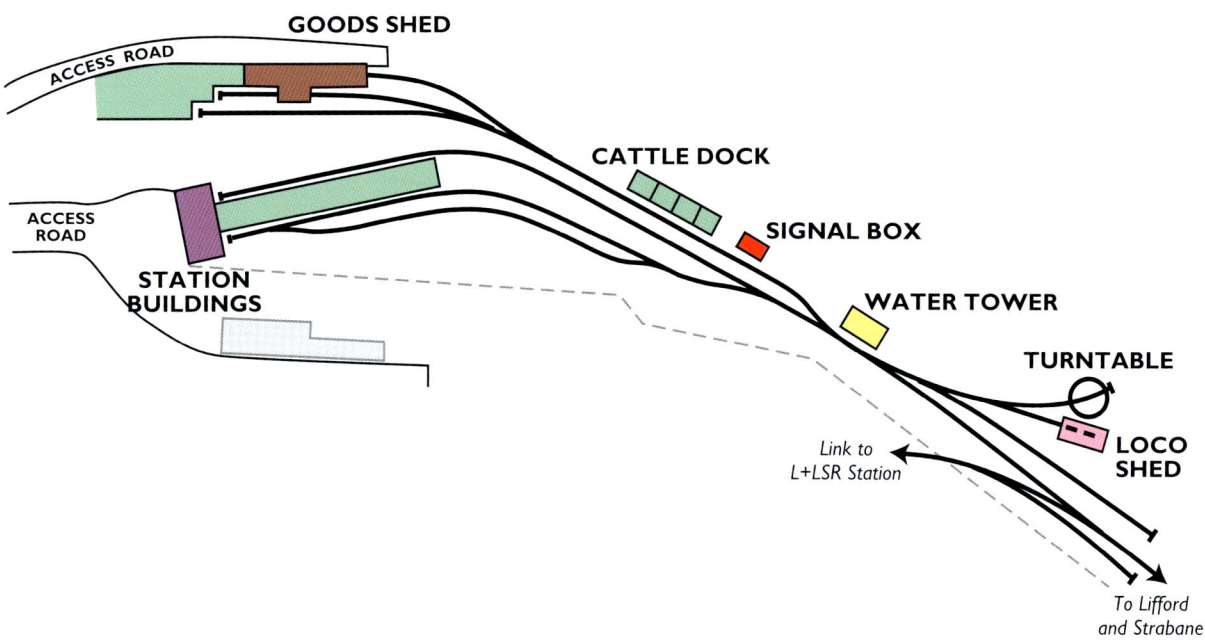

A very typical midday scene at Letterkenny with No 1 *Alice* 'ready to go' with a train for Stranorlar on 19 May 1956. The loco is well coaled and the guard will be just talking things through with the driver. In the right centre background the roof of Oatfield's sweet factory can be seen and the yellow building in the background is the original 1909 station, still standing and now the headquarters of Bus Éireann for Letterkenny and part of the Donegal area. The spire of the Cathedral towers above the station roof. There was a big oil company in Letterkenny called the Donegal Oil Company and the barrels on the platform are possibly traffic for them. The flat wagon behind the locomotive would most probably have been converted from an old coach chassis and used to convey a variety of loads. The Lough Swilly station was over to the left and there was a link through the goods sidings between the two networks, although by this time the Swilly had closed, having ceased running to Letterkenny in 1953.

ES Russell/ColourRail

No 16 railcar arrives at Letterkenny on 19 May 1956 with the 11.20 from Strabane and is almost dwarfed by the amount of freight traffic that is evident. The telegraph poles lying in the foreground have been previously unloaded from the flat wagon. The water tower is in the background and the Swilly station and yard is out of view to the right. The coach behind No 16 is probably corridor third No 30, built in 1901 by Oldbury. She later was fitted out with bucket seats, and even roller bearings, to work with railcars on the Letterkenny line.

ES Russell/ColourRail

Letterkenny station front is seen, complete with an early series Donegal-registered (ZP) Morris Minor. The stationmaster's house is to the left. The crest over the station entrance proudly displays the opening date of 1909. The white wall of the Swilly Station can also just be seen on the right.

K Bannister/ColourRail

23

CASTLEFINN

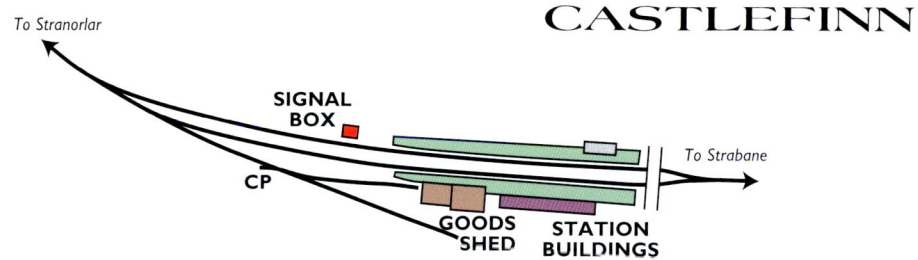

STRANORLAR

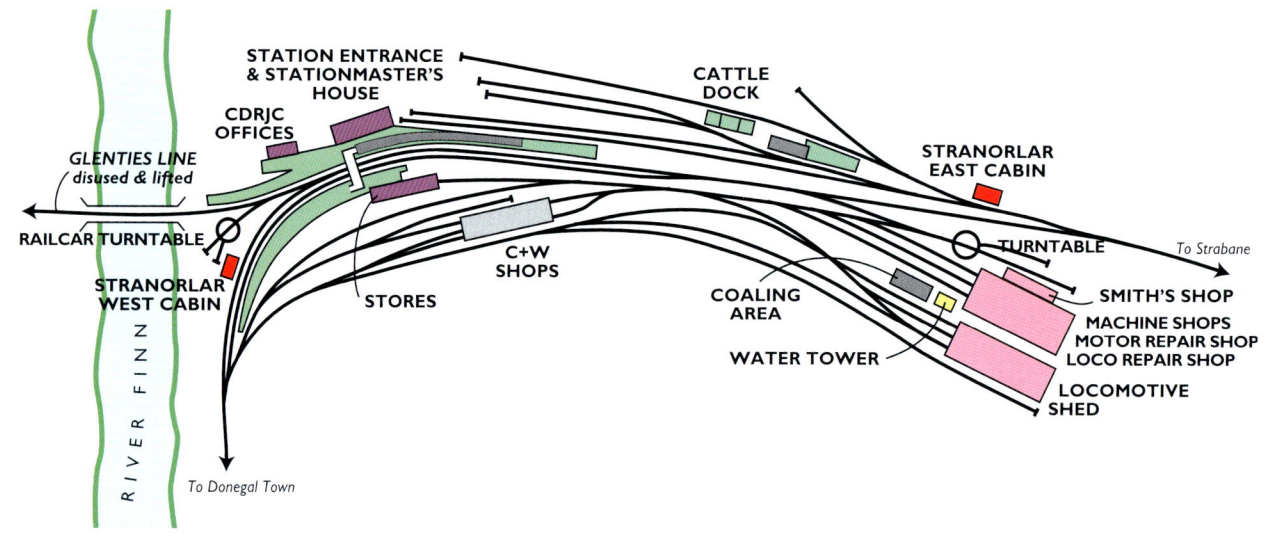

DONEGAL

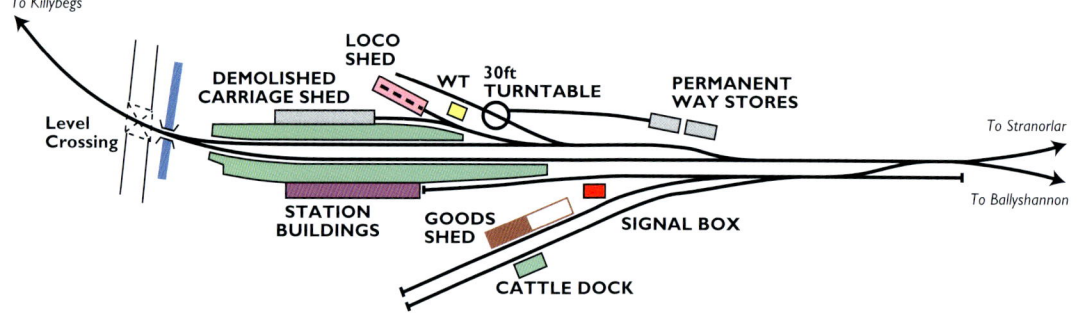

Turning to the Finn Valley route, No 4 *Meenglas* runs into Castlefinn at midday on 18 June 1959. This is a typical mixed train with a guards van and even a red wagon attached. Castlefinn was another customs post and wagons would be recessed here for customs clearance. As with Strabane, passenger trains were also checked here and cleared through the border by means of trestle tables for examining luggage. The box on the platform is one from Jacob's Biscuits which were transported in small containers. To speed up customs clearance, trains could work up from Strabane and leave a train of wagons recessed in the sidings to the left for checking. The engine would then take a train back to Strabane or run back light. Also, customs clearance papers would be sent on from Strabane on an earlier railcar, allowing customs officers to check papers before the goods train arrived and be ready to inspect anything they wanted to in advance. Originally 5'3" gauge, the Finn Valley route was converted to narrow gauge by 16 July 1894 and the space between the platforms illustrates this. The signal cabin stands guard over the scene; there were two signalmen based here who were also porters to help with baggage during customs clearance and to help with mails.

AG Cramp/ColourRail

No 2 *Blanche* leaves Stranorlar with Francie McMenamin on the footplate and is seen near Town Bridge Halt with a freight for Strabane on 13 August 1957. The gable of the goods store and Stranorlar East signal box can be seen in the background through the smoke. The two jacks can be seen on the front of the locomotive. Town Bridge Halt was not a popular halt, it being opened in 1934 and closed in the early 1950s.

C Hogg/ColourRail

25

No 18 railcar, driven by Paddy Hannigan, arrives at Stranorlar on 22 May 1956. To the right is a flat roofed building with a green door, which is the blacksmiths. This employed three blacksmiths and three strikers who made many things for the railway, including springs and buffers. The cranes on this side were often used for lifting wagons, coaches and railcars during maintenance – 40 men were employed in total in these works. To the left is the goods loading bank where another crane was used to load and unload wagons. The goods covered up are probably building materials awaiting collection by a local builder. On the signal post is an acetylene gas lamp of a rather classical style, but it was not an unusual feature as there was a gas tank here that was used to top up the tanks on some of the earlier coaches that had gas lights. This system was extended to the station. Paddy went on to become a bus inspector when the CDRJC became a total road operator.

ES Russell/ColourRail

Looking in the other direction, No 11 *Erne* is seen at Stranorlar East. The goods store is on the right and the fine gantry signal and light is evident. The building to the left with the green door is the carpenters' shops, outside of which lies a pile of sleepers, probably salvaged from the closed line to Glenties. A rake of coaches sitting on the back roads were stored for excursions; some have doors open so they were probably being made ready for use. The three coaches nearest to the platform are the Ballycastle coaches Nos 57, 58 and 59 which were purchased from the UTA in 1950 for £1,399. Stranorlar was the headquarters of the CDRJC and the offices were situated in the building with the clock tower. A tractor can just be seen between the locomotive and the goods shed – a farmer has come to collect something. The goods shed was always very busy and in good condition. Unfortunately, not much in this photograph survives, but the two faces of the station clock have been preserved and are now on a new plinth in front of the church which was opened for the new Millennium on 1 January 2000. The date here is some 44 years earlier on 22 May 1956.

ES Russell/ColourRail

A general view of Stranorlar station in 1950. Eason's bookstall is seen, and the man walking down the line towards the photographer is the General Foreman of all the works, Johnnie Kelly. Stored coaches can be seen again awaiting the next excursion. To the left is the tractor *Phoenix* which has made it up from Strabane. This locomotive, although latterly more associated with Strabane, worked in Stranorlar for years as the shunting engine. It may be here for routine maintenance or has perhaps worked a train of wagons up from Strabane. It looks like Danny Montieth, its regular driver, is on the locomotive, so it would be in working order. The magnificent station buildings, that carried the Finn Valley crest with its motto 'Be Just and Fear Not', have unfortunately been demolished.

WHG Boot/ColourRail

No 2 *Blanche* stands at Stranorlar with a mixed train on 19 May 1956. The first three coaches are the Ballycastle ones which, together with a CDR vehicle, are most likely being moved to Strabane for an excursion. Behind these are an oil tanker, while another tanker stands over to the left in the siding. Then follows a number of general goods wagons, the last one in view being a cattle wagon. The carpenters' shops can be seen once again, while the next door up is the general stores.

ES Russell/ColourRail

The date is 22 May 1956 and coach repairs are seen underway at Stranorlar. This area was called 'The Graveyard'. Here coaches would be cannibalised to keep others going; the one nearest the camera seems to have already given up some window glasses, whilst the next one seems to have been lifted off its bogies. The acetylene tank for lighting can clearly be seen on the end of the near coach. The man walking towards the camera is John Maneely. In the bottom right-hand corner is the end of a flat wagon with 'I.A.O. Co. Ltd.' written on it. This was a vehicle for the Irish American Oil Company and would, at one time, have had a tank on the top of it.

ES Russell/ColourRail

No 4 *Meenglas* is seen at Stranorlar on 8 May 1957. Out of sight behind the water tower is the running shed; The three buildings with pitched roofs are, from left to right, the machine shop, the railcar running shed and the locomotive repair shop, where heavy overhauls were carried out, The machine shop had all the lathes, wheel turners and brass turners operated by skilled men. Over to the left is the turntable and the wagon by the side of this is the breakdown van No 1. This was always loaded with jacks, timbers, sledge hammers and the like, and could be on the move very quickly. Certain men from the workshops were dedicated to be its crew.

ColourRail

Roughly two years later, on 22 June 1959, No 4 *Meenglas* and No 11 *Erne* pose outside the running shed at Stranorlar. It looks as though *Erne* is not in steam and has been dragged out for inspection. An enthusiasts' visit is clearly in progress as evidenced by the presence of cameras.

ColourRail

No 14 railcar and trailer No 3 plus three red wagons are seen at Stranorlar on 4 August 1958. Trailer No 3 had been converted from No 3 railcar, an eight-wheeler purchased from the Dublin and Blessington Steam Tramway. As a railcar it was unique on 'The Donegal' as it could be driven from both ends without the need for turning. It was converted to a trailer in 1944 at Stranorlar and can now be found in the Ulster Folk and Transport Museum.

ES Russell/ColourRail

On this occasion the photographer is standing on the platform that was adjacent to the stub end of the former line to Glenties which diverged from Stranorlar at this point. No 2 *Blanche* is seen preparing to leave with a goods for Donegal on 8 May 1959. The back of a No 10 railcar, going in the Strabane direction, can be seen, as can the footbridge that spanned the lines here. The enamel signs for 'Virol' and 'Stranorlar' can be seen, with Eason's bookstall (they also had stalls at Strabane and Letterkenny) just to the left of the Virol sign. No 10 railcar has a white tailboard on it, indicating the end of the train.

JG Dewing/ColourRail

A busy scene at Stranorlar West is glimpsed on 22 June 1959 from the footbridge at the station. The picture shows No 4 *Meenglas* with Ballycastle coach No 58 and part of the first wagon of a freight train (which had a passenger coach attached to it for the enthusiasts); No 16 railcar and wagon waiting to go to Donegal town and Killybegs; and No 20 railcar arriving from Killybegs. This is the same date as the previous photograph of *Meenglas* and *Erne*, outside the running shed at Stranorlar (page 29, top), definitely some sort of enthusiasts' visit. Note the luggage rack on top of No 16 – these were generally only used for bicycles and there was quite a technique involved in getting one up and then back down! The gentleman in the left-hand corner of the photograph is Donald Feeley, one of the clerical officers at Stranorlar. The track to the right was the stub of the line to Glenties, closed to regular services from December 1947.

ColourRail

Looking from the closed Glenties formation across where the now demolished bridge once stood over the River Finn, the Stranorlar West signal cabin and railcar trailer No 3 can be seen at Stranorlar station. Note the 'STOP' sign in the foreground which seems to have survived, only having lost its 'S'. The brown, wooden building on the back of the signal cabin was the store for the signal fitters.

K Bannister/ColourRail

DONEGAL

No 2 *Blanche* and No 19 railcar are seen at Donegal town on 3 August 1959. *Blanche* has arrived on the train on the left and is running round to access the Ballyshannon line. Note the water tower behind the locomotive. The engine driver is Jim McKenna and the gentleman looking into No 19 railcar is Collins Lafferty, the railcar having just come off the 30' turntable. The turntable was essential as it was used to turn railcars working the Ballyshannon trains.

ES Russell/ColourRail

No 16 railcar is seen at Donegal on a cold 8 March 1958. The railcar driver is Joe Thompson and No 16 is forming a train for Ballyshannon. Two grey wagons and two lighter, red wagons, that were designed for railcar use, make up the train. Behind the railcar is the former locomotive running shed. This train would be waiting for connections from Killybegs and Strabane.

ColourRail

A general view of Donegal town looking towards Killybegs on 30 May 1957. Happily the buildings here are still intact, but the footbridge and most of the platforms have gone. Two grey wagons have been left in the platform road for collection or shunting, usually carried out by a railcar. Just visible, lurking in the goods store, is the back of a GNR bus which was used to connect with trains to Portnoo.

FW Shuttleworth/ColourRail

The approach to Donegal town from the east, together with the magnificent signal gantries, is seen with the Ballyshannon line to the left and the Stranorlar line to the right. In the distance is the station with a railcar trailer, possibly No 5, in the back siding next to the water tower. To the left is the goods store and to the left of that is possibly Magee's tweed factory. Today the County Donegal Railway Restoration Society has a Heritage Centre here, the intention being to rebuild some of the railway and operate the original locomotives, railcars and rolling stock.

K Bannister/ColourRail

Looking from the platform roads towards the east, this photograph was taken at Donegal town on 30 May 1957. The Ballyshannon line diverges to the right, Stranorlar to the left and the fine array of signals can be viewed. Donegal cabin can be seen to the right in immaculate condition, complete with concrete steps as most of the CDR cabins seemed to have had at this time. From right to left the roads are: goods store; a platform siding where some Ballyshannon services started; the two through platform roads; the road to the former carriage shed that ran alongside the platform; the road to the loco shed; and the road to the turntable, water tower and permanent way stores. Note too the red ground signal, interlocked with the point rodding which controlled access from the turntable road.

FW Shuttleworth/ColourRail

33

Further over to the left on the same date (30 May 1957), a closer view of the water tower, former locomotive shed and platform siding is pictured. The siding was once partly covered by a carriage shed from approximately where the photographer is standing. The fine starting signals on the platform ends can also be seen. Two railcar wagons and an open wagon – used mainly for coal or permanent way materials – can be seen standing on this road and another covered wagon waits in the siding to the right.

FW Shuttleworth/ColourRail

Looking to the right from the same position, on the same date, we see goods wagons in both the platform road and the yard. The open wagons seem to have sleepers in and were obviously being used on permanent way works. Another wagon can be seen poking out of the goods store and the crane is seen in the background, next to the cattle dock.

FW Shuttleworth/ColourRail

No 2 *Blanche* waits at Donegal town on 19 May 1956 with a goods service that contains four passenger coaches. These would either be empty stock being re-positioned, or extra coaches laid on in connection with the Killybegs Regatta. Sam Oliphant is doing the driving. Note the tanker wagon, which would be returning to Strabane from Killybegs, behind the last of the four coaches, the first three being the rather luxurious Ballycastle set. Other extra trains ran to Killybegs on 15 August every year and were known as the '15th August Excursions'. The turntable, with railcar wagons and other wagons, can be seen to the right. We will see this train again later on in the book in the freight section, on page 105.
ES Russell/ColourRail

No 12 railcar has arrived at Donegal town on 3 August 1959. Forming a Killybegs service, it also has a carriage coupled to it – one of the Strabane and Letterkenny vehicles – and a trailer. No 12 was introduced in 1934 and seated 41 passengers. It was the first railcar built for the CDR with the Walker Brothers' power bogie. By this time there were only five months of rail services left, but the company replaced these rail services 'like for like' with road transport for both passengers and freight from 1 January 1960.
ES Russell/ColourRail

35

Taken from the footbridge, No 4 *Meenglas* is seen running round a freight at Donegal town on 22 June 1959. The rear coach is one of the Ballycastle coaches – No 58. This is the train we saw earlier at Stranorlar West (page 30) with the additional coach full of enthusiasts. Maybe they had had a coach added so that they could have a steam-hauled trip through the Barnesmore Gap. The locomotive is about to shunt some wagons to and from the train and then proceed on to Killybegs. The Ballycastle coaches were originally corridor connected and the blanked off panel can be seen here. The passenger van is just seen at the other end of the train. The crate on the platform probably contains machinery for Magees of Donegal town.

ColourRail

No 19 railcar, driven by Eddie Sweeney, leaves Donegal town on a Killybegs train on 22 June 1959. This was not the usual platform for a Killybegs departure, that being on the adjacent line.

ColourRail

On the Killybegs road at Inver three members of staff are seen on the platform. Christie Kennedy, the motorman of the railcar (out of sight), is identified by red flashes on his lapels; the man in the centre is Neil Ward, the stationmaster; and the third, unidentified man is a member of the post office. Although unseen, a railcar has already been recessed into the siding here, to cross another, the siding points starting from just behind where the photographer is standing. The entrance to the station can be seen by the lamp on the platform and the enamel sign 'Inver' is also visible.

K Bannister/ColourRail

KILLYBEGS

Nos 19 and 14 railcars arrive at Killybegs on 3 August 1959. The line hugged the edge of Killybegs bay at this point, the line to the right originally leading to the locomotive shed, by then demolished. There was some art in driving two railcars at once, as both were independently operated. There is also a trailer on the rear of the train.

ES Russell/ColourRail

KILLYBEGS

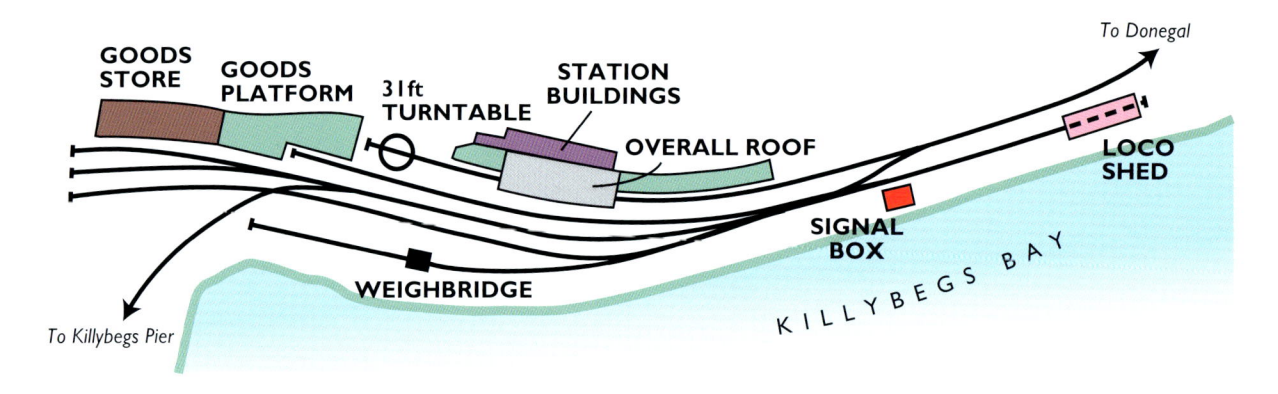

Malinmore — Killybegs Routes

		WEEK-DAYS			S.O.	SUN-DAYS
		a.m.	p.m.	p.m.	p.m.	a.m.
MALINMORE	dep.	8. 0	2. 0	5.50	—	10.30
GLENCOLUMBKILLE	,,	8.15	2.15	6. 5	—	10.50
CARRICK	,,	8.40	2.40	6.30	8.30	
KILCAR	,,	8.55	2.55	6.45	8.45	
KILLYBEGS	arr.	9.25	3.25	7.15	9.15	

				S.O.	S.E.	S.O.
		a.m.	p.m.	p.m.	p.m.	p.m.
KILLYBEGS	dep.	11. 0	4.20	7.20	7.55	9.30
KILCAR	,,	11.30	4.50	7.50	8.25	10. 0
CARRICK	,,	11.45	5. 5	8. 5	8.40	10.15	Noon
GLENCOLUMBKILLE	,,	12.10	5.30	—	9. 5	10.40	12. 0
MALINMORE	arr.	12.25	5.45	—	9.20	10.55	12.20

S.O.— SATURDAYS ONLY.   S.E.— SATURDAYS EXCEPTED.

Timetable for connecting bus service from Killybegs to Malinmore

A photograph taken roughly two years earlier than the previous one on 30 May 1957, sees a railcar shunting at Killybegs. This also shows the former engine shed and a shunter to the right who is operating the points. The railcars, as well as being much cheaper to operate than steam locomotives on passenger services, were also able to pull goods wagons to good effect and their ability to perform shunting duties between their passenger workings made the economics of working the CDR more efficient. This must have been why the CDR managed to continue to operate as a railway operator as long as it did – with only the West Clare managing to beat the longevity of its rail operations on the Irish narrow gauge. Note that the engine shed was damaged by No 6 *Columbkille* and had to be demolished – hence the difference between these last two photographs!

FW Shuttleworth/ColourRail

No 14 railcar pokes out of the train shed (which kept out the biting Atlantic gales) at Killybegs. The pier can be seen in the background, where CDRJC lines (still partly extant) went out onto the pier for traffic associated with the fishing fleet – an important customer. A permanent way gang carries out the important task of track maintenance in front of the railcar – it also looks as thought they are being helped by a couple of boys! The date was 19 August 1958.

ColourRail

39

Killybegs station is seen from the edge of the turntable looking towards Donegal on 19 August 1958. No 14 railcar is demonstrating its worth by shunting some wagons, including an open wagon with what looks like some sort of machinery – maybe for the fishing fleet. The water tower (still standing) and column can be seen to the left of the platform, and the permanent way gang are still hard at work.

The turntable here followed the well-know 'waste not, want not' policy of the CDR, being constructed from the frames of former 2-6-4 tank No 19 *Letterkenny* in 1950. Before this, it had been the frames of an original Class 2 4-6-0 tank that had been used.

ColourRail

Trailer No 5 and a red wagon are seen being turned on the aforementioned turntable at Killybegs on 3 August 1959. This photograph perfectly illustrates the loco frame construction of the turntable. Trailer No 5 was supplied as a trailer in 1929, with a Knutsford Motors-built chassis and coachwork by O'Dohertys. It seated 28 people and on closure was sold to Donegal Football Club and later became a hen house. Happily she is now at Donegal town station undergoing restoration. The red wagons were derived from other railways, No 1 was the breakdown van, No 2 was a covered ex-Clogher Valley wagon, Nos 3 to 9 were flats from the Castlederg and Victoria Bridge Tramway, and Nos 10 to 23 were all covered and came from the Clogher Valley.

ES Russell/ColourRail

AEC Regal IV, No 271, Model No 9822E with GNR bodywork on a Park Royal chassis with pre-select gear box, waits at Killybegs on 3 August 1959. Here there was a road connection to Malinmore and Glencolumbkille (see Timetable on page 38). Behind is a CDR Leyland Beaver.

Killybegs was an important base for lorries, as all of the fish that were caught late evening and overnight were put onto CDR lorries and transported to Dublin every night of the week.

ES Russell/ColourRail

A pleasant view of Rossnowlagh taken on 23 June 1959. Behind the platform was a turntable to turn railcars employed on what was the only scheduled Sunday service on the CDR. It ran from Ballyshannon to Rossnowlagh for services at Rossnowlagh Priory, built in the mid 1940s. The train left Ballyshannon at 10.30 am, arriving at Rossnowlagh at 10.50 am. It then returned at 12.00 pm, arriving at Ballyshannon at 12.20 pm. The stationmaster's house here still stands today.

ES Russell/ColourRail

No 18 railcar is seen on a Sunday working, being turned on the table at Rossnowlagh. This turntable was originally sited at Londonderry Victoria Road. The date was 16 August 1959. The inset illustration shows the privilege ticket issued to John Langford on this occasion.

John Langford

No 2 *Blanche* is seen at Rossnowlagh, looking towards Donegal town on 3 August 1959. On this occasion *Blanche* had hauled an excursion in from Strabane and had been shunting two coaches into the siding here. These were probably for Rossnowlagh passengers. The track into the turntable can just be seen to the left, a little overgrown.

ES Russell/ColourRail

No 2 *Blanche* arrives at Ballyshannon on 3 August 1959 with a bank holiday excursion. The centre signal on the gantry is off for the platform road, and the carriages seem to be filled with eager passengers! There seem to be some very large lumps of coal in the bunker, which the fireman will no doubt have fun breaking up later on! Once the train was empty, the carriages would be recessed to the sidings on the right by the signal cabin.

ES Russell/ColourRail

No 5 *Drumboe* of 1907 vintage makes a fine sight at Ballyshannon on 4 August 1958 as she takes water from the column. To the rear is the station platform and there are many wagons by the goods store which is just out of the picture.

ES Russell/ColourRail

43

Ballyshannon on 30 May 1957, with No 15 railcar having backed up a wagon of timber to the goods store. This was probably for the big builders' merchants Myles who were based in Ballyshannon. Railcar motorman Joe Thompson is walking back towards the cab. Once again the railcar illustrates its worth as a 'Jack of all trades'. Also, a railcar trailer, this time No 2, is stabled in the yard waiting to be turned. This was originally railcar No 2 and came from the Castlederg and Victoria Bridge Tramway. Introduced on the CDR in 1934, she replaced the earlier No 2 which had come in during the Forbes era back in 1926, originally having worked on the Derwent Valley line in England.

FW Shuttleworth/ColourRail

This is another nice Ballyshannon photograph, taken on the same date. No 15 railcar has just reversed into a siding and is in process of being turned. Trailer No 2 awaits its turn after some shunting. A good number of wagons wait by the goods store, the open ones being loaded with coal. To the rear of the railcar is the locomotive shed; the white-faced platform to the left of the railcar is the cattle dock.

FW Shuttleworth/ColourRail

Two years later, Ballyshannon is seen on 23 June 1959, this time showing the stationmaster's house and the station buildings. The very long platform here illustrates the fact that many long excursions ran to and from Ballyshannon. Inspection of the track layout will reveal a number of long sidings to cope with these. The number of wagons here shows that freight traffic was still buoyant despite the fact that closure was to occur in only six months' time.

ColourRail

BALLYSHANNON

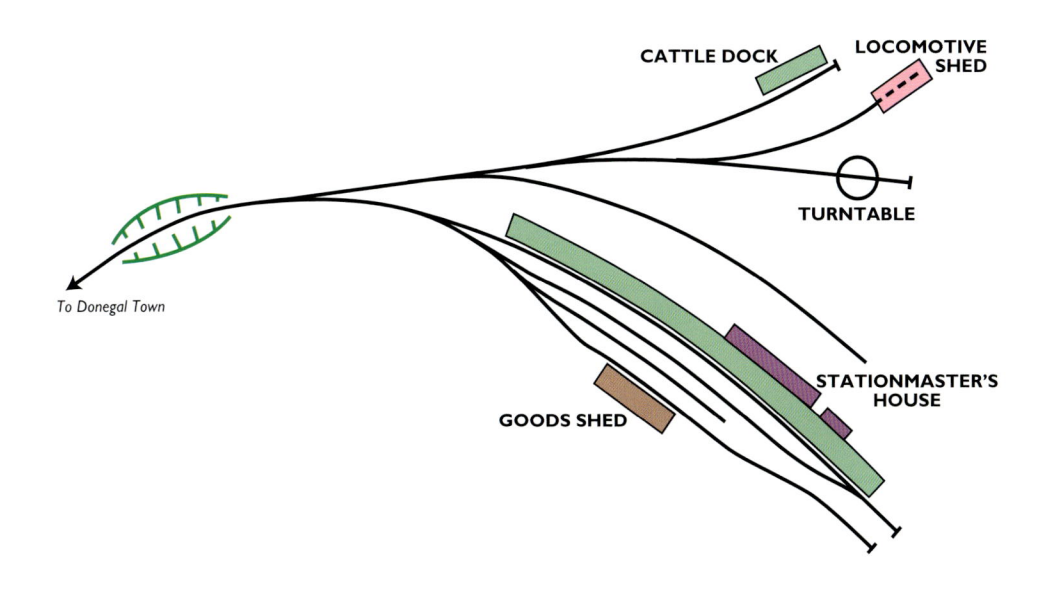

Class 5A 2-6-4 tank locomotive　Scale: 6 mm to 1 ft

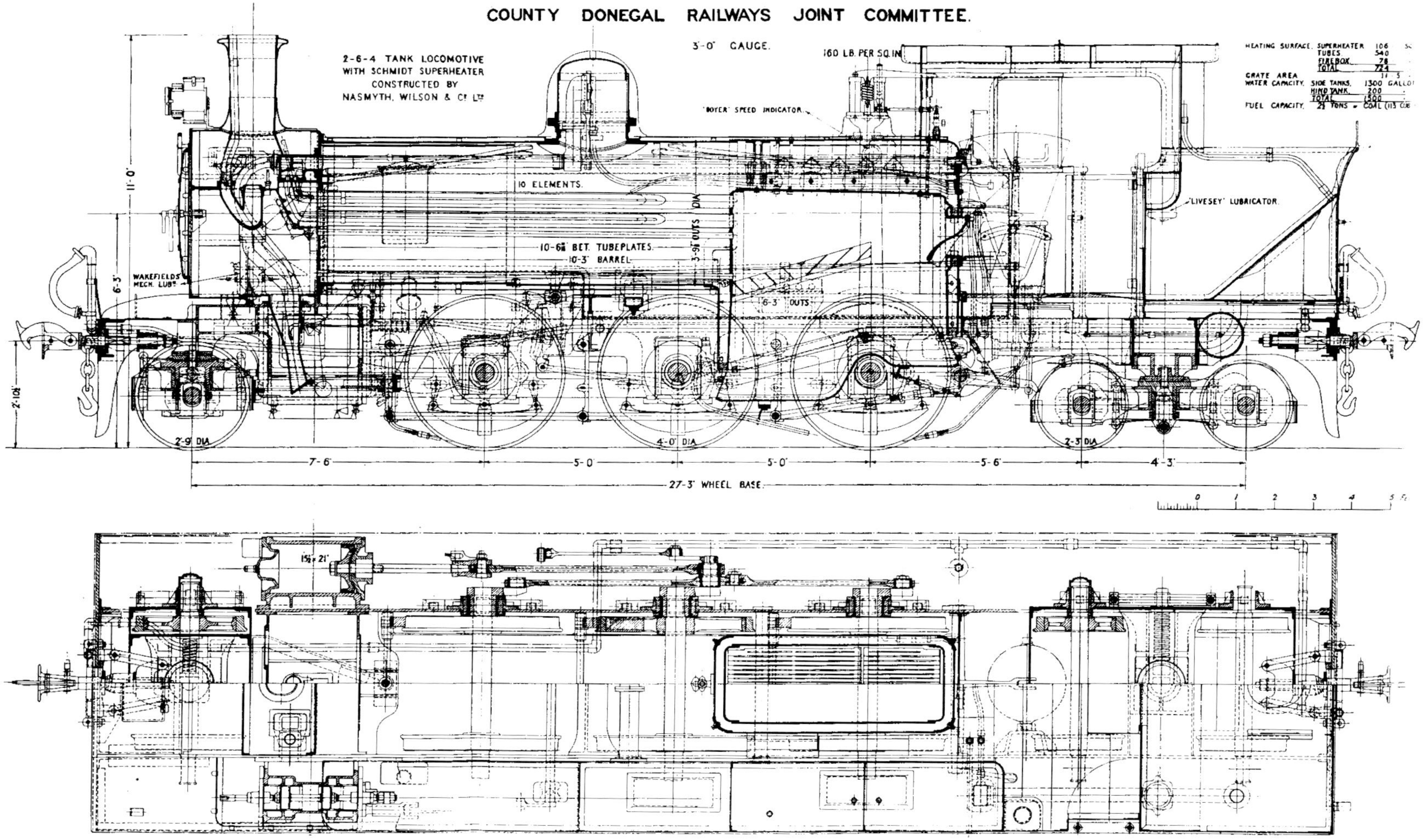

STEAM LOCOMOTIVES

The steam locomotives featured in this book are the surviving 'modern' Class 4, 5 and 5A types which were produced for the CDRJC from 1904. The original Finn Valley standard gauge service that ran from Strabane to Stranorlar used locomotives hired from the Irish North Western, latterly the Great Northern. The 3'0" gauge West Donegal from Stranorlar to Donegal utilised three 2-4-0 Class 1 tank locomotives: No 1 *Alice*, No 2 *Blanche* and No 3 *Lydia*, built in 1881 by Sharp, Stewart and Company. As the 3'0" gauge expanded, six more locomotives, this time of Class 2 classification and 4-6-0 tank arrangement, came from Neilson and Company in 1893. These were No 4 *Meenglas*, No 5 *Drumboe*, No 6 *Inver*, No 7 *Finn*, No 8 *Foyle* and No 9 *Columbkille*. As traffic grew, two 4-4-4 tanks from Neilson, Reid of Class 3 type were introduced in 1902, these being No 10 *Sir James* and No 11 *Hercules*. These both lasted until 1933.

The large Class 4, 5 and 5A locomotives of 4-6-4 and 2-6-4 wheel arrangement were all introduced between 1904 and 1912 and were all built by Nasmyth, Wilson. With the possible exception of the two Lough Swilly 4-8-4 tank locomotives that were built for the Burtonport extension, these locomotives were certainly amongst the most impressive and powerful 3'0" narrow gauge tank locomotives ever built. The red livery of the CDRJC certainly seemed to enhance their appearance and it is good to know that some have survived the breaker's torch. Classes 4 and 5 were later superheated and both classes 5 and 5A were renumbered and renamed as the older classes 1, 2 and 3 were withdrawn due to railcars assuming all the non-excursion passenger work.

A Class 5A 2–6–4 tank locomotive. **Scale: 4 mm to 1 ft**

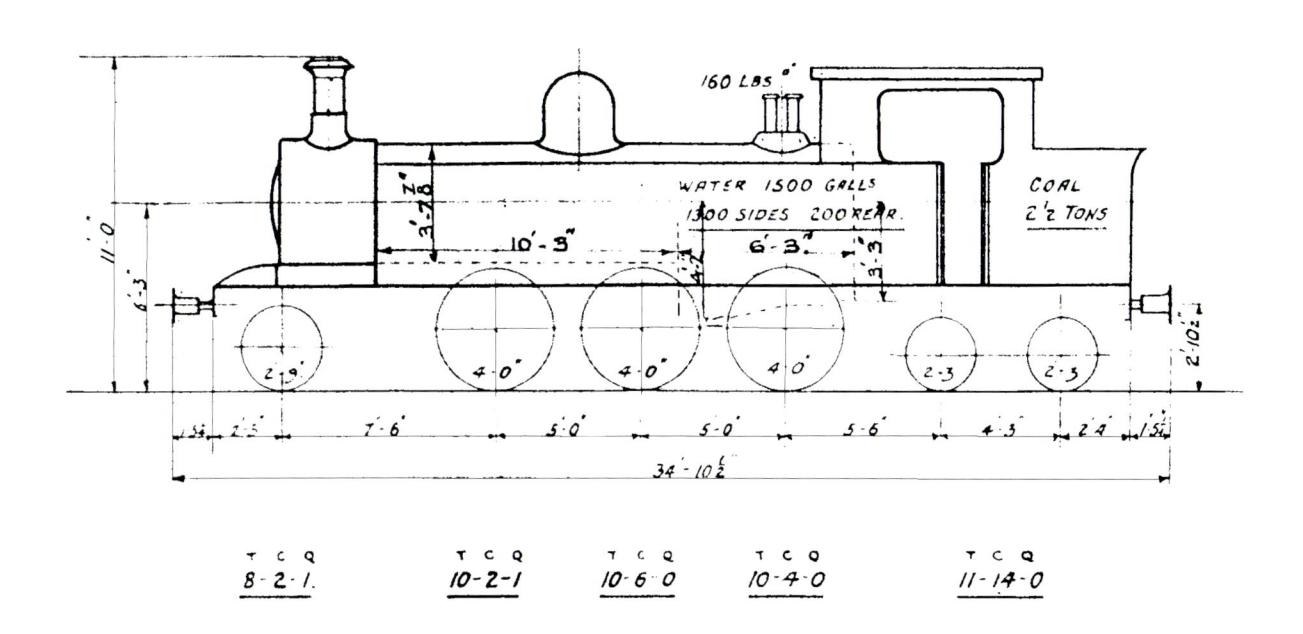

47

Class 5A 2-6-4 tank No 1 *Alice* is seen at Strabane in July 1954. The Class 5A locomotives, of which there were three, were introduced in 1912. They had greater water capacity – initially 1,500 gallons – with longer side tanks than the Class 5s. Two hundred gallons of this total was held in a small tank in the bunker – this was later removed, which increased the coal capacity. The three locomotives were all superheated from new, unlike the other CDR engines, and had piston valves and large bore cylinders, Wakefield mechanical lubricators, and automatic lubrication for axles and bogies. They even carried speedometers. The line behind *Alice* continued to Derry and the trans-ship shed can be seen in the background along with another locomotive shunting wagons. Note the small ground signal that was controlled from Strabane cabin and protected the main line from the sidings.

AD Hutchinson/ColourRail

No 1 *Alice* seen again at Strabane in July 1954. Built by Nasmyth, Wilson, she was maker's number 958. However, she did not start off as *Alice*, as there was another earlier locomotive carrying that name – a Sharp Stewart 2-4-0 tank which was eventually scrapped in 1926. *Alice* was originally numbered No 21 and was named *Ballyshannon*. She was renumbered in 1927 as No 1 and named *Alice* a year later. Unfortunately she was sold for scrap on 1 March 1961 after a period in store at Stranorlar shed. To the rear is an M2 van on the GN side and the shunting locomotive can just be seen in the yard to the left of the signal.

AD Hutchinson/ColourRail

Class 5A No 2 *Blanche* is seen being coupled to a train at Donegal on 19 May 1956. The 2-6-4 wheel arrangement is well illustrated along with the extended water tanks that come right up to the smokebox – the Class 5s has shorter tanks. It is obviously an excursion day as there is other coaching stock in the 'back road' here. *Blanche*, of 1912 vintage, was Nasmyth, Wilson builder's number 956 and originally CDR No 2A *Strabane*. She was re-numbered No 2 and re-named *Blanche* in 1928 – the previous locomotive to have carried this name being a Sharp, Stewart 2-4-0T which had been scrapped in 1909.

ES Russell/ColourRail

A fine photograph for comparative purposes shows Class 5 No 4 *Meenglas* and Class 5A No 2 *Blanche* at Strabane on 4 August 1959. The main difference was the length of the water tanks, No 2's extending to the smokebox and No 4's being much shorter. Francie McMenamin is seen on the footplate of No 4. In the background is Douglas Iron Works, which became part of the Hammond Lane Foundry. Happily both these locomotives survived, No 4 at the Foyle Valley Railway and No 2 at the Belfast Transport Museum, before going on to the Ulster Folk and Transport Museum at Cultra.

ES Russell/ColourRail

A Class 5 2–6–4 tank locomotive.

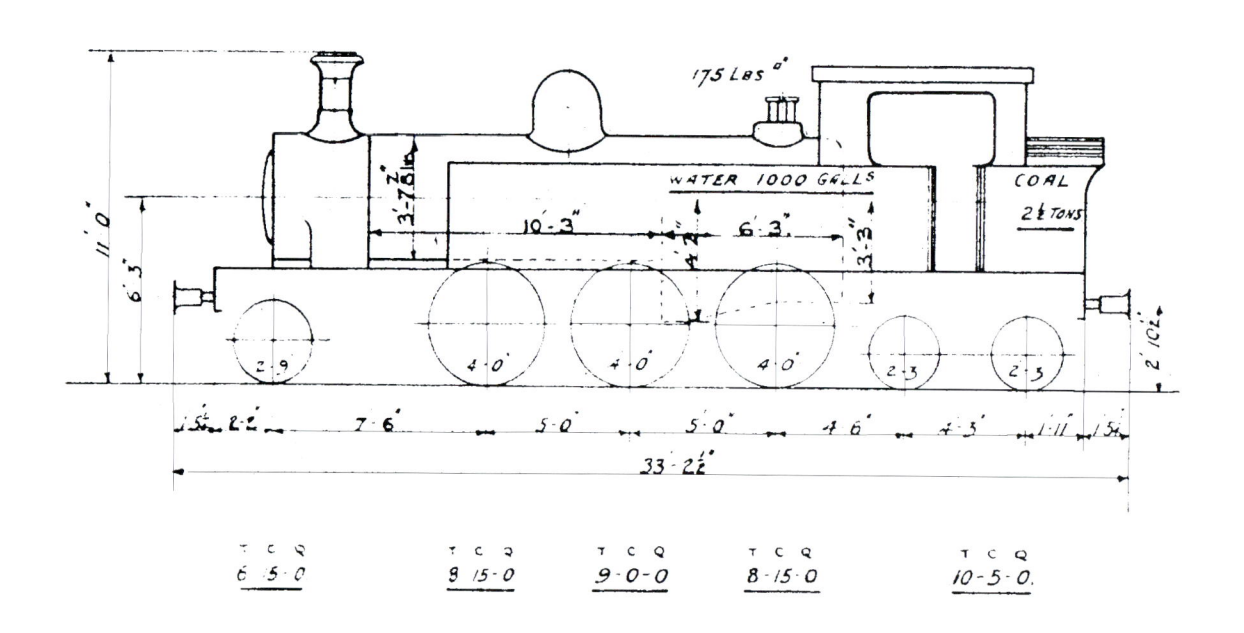

Scale: 4 mm to 1 ft

The third of the class 5As was No 3 *Lydia*, seen at Strabane in June 1952. This locomotive was Nasmyth, Wilson builder's number 957 and was originally CDR No 3A *Stranorlar*, being re-numbered and re-named in 1928. The three Class 5A locomotives weighed 50 tons 8 cwt and had a boiler pressure of 160 lbs. With 4'0" driving wheels and 15"x21" cylinders they had a massive tractive effort of 14,294.8 lbs. They cost £2,495 each. *Lydia* was sold for scrap with her sister *Alice* on 1 March 1961 after a public auction.

I Davidson/ColourRail

The first of the Class 5s to be introduced in 1907 was 2-6-4 tank locomotive No 16 *Donegal*. She was built by Nasmyth, Wilson and was their works number 828. Originally unsuperheated, the five members of the class were capable of matching the Class 4 'Baltics', but they were better steamers. They were also more economical on coal, according to the then Chief Engineer on the CDR, RM Livesey. Originally saturated, they were fitted with superheaters and, as earlier locomotives were withdrawn, re-named and re-numbered. No 16 was superheated in 1926 and became No 4 *Meenglas* in 1937, a name and number originally carried by a 4-6-0 tank locomotive scrapped in 1935. She is seen at Ballyshannon on 3 August 1959, a day of excursions. The signal is off for another arrival that was hauled by No 2 *Blanche*.

ES Russell/ColourRail

No 4 *Meenglas* is seen again, with Francie McMenamin in the cab, this time at Stranorlar running shed on 31 July 1959. This view illustrates the wheel arrangement and shorter water tanks of the Class 5s when compared to the Class 5As. The wagon on the left is No 1 red wagon – the breakdown van. *Meenglas* was purchased by Dr Cox on closure, but due to the aforementioned problems with shipping costs she was stored at Strabane before going to the Foyle Valley Railway in Derry.

B Hilton/ColourRail

51

A 'side on' view of No 4 *Meenglas* on Ballyshannon turntable on 3 August 1959. No 18 railcar is in the background, with its driver Joe Thompson in the navy blue suit helping to turn the locomotive. Note the polished triangular builders plate, the re-railing jacks, and the fine CDR crest on the bunker. The signal is still in the 'off' position.

ES Russell/ColourRail

Class 5 No 5 *Drumboe* is seen with a goods at Strabane on 2 August 1959. Jim McMenamin, the brother of Francie, stands on the locomotive. She has arrived at Strabane, has run round and looks to be propelling back into the goods sidings and the trans-ship. The inevitable passenger van is next to the engine. *Drumboe* was originally No 17 *Glenties*, Nasmyth, Wilson No 829, and was superheated in 1929. She was also purchased in 1961 by Dr Cox for his scheme but thankfully now resides at Donegal town.

ES Russell/ColourRail

No 5 *Drumboe* has arrived at Castlefinn with a goods for Stranorlar on 23 June 1959. Francie McMenamin is on the footplate. A train of wagons to the right is recessed, probably for customs clearance, and the red wagon on the back of train on the left denotes it is a railcar service. However, there is no sign of the white plate on the back that would indicate the end of the train, so either the sign is not quite in the photograph or there is shunting going on.

The McMenamin brothers were probably the most famous of the CDR's loco crews. Towards the end of the line, Francie, the driver, turned 65 years old, and brother Jim would have been about 61. The age limit for drivers on the CDR was 65, so they, in theory, 'swopped sides' on the locomotive with Francie becoming the fireman and Jim the driver. In fact, they probably just carried on as they always had done!

ColourRail

No 6 *Columbkille* is seen at Strabane shunting wagons near the trans-shipment shed. No 6 was originally No 18 *Killybegs* and was introduced in 1907. Builder's number 830, she became No 6 *Columbkille* in 1937, after being superheated in 1925. Again, she was brought by Dr Cox, but despite languishing at Strabane, survived to join No 4 *Meenglas* in beautiful condition at the Foyle Valley Railway in Derry. The Class 5 specifications were: 4'0" driving wheels; boiler pressure, 175 lbs; water capacity, 1,000 gallons; coal capacity, 2 tons; weight, 43 tons 10 cwt; tractive effort, 12,755.4 lbs. They cost the CDR £2,475 each. There seems to be a lucky visitor in the cab. The date is July 1954.

AD Hutchinson/ColourRail

No 7 *Finn* (although the locomotive never carried the number or name!) was the next in numerical line, originally having been introduced in 1908 as No 19 *Letterkenny*. She was builder's number 831. She was involved in the serious accident at Donemana on 7 September 1913, and although superheated in 1929 was scrapped in 1940. Her frames were later used to form the turntable at Killybegs (see page 40). The next Class 5 in line order was No 8 *Foyle* and this fine locomotive is seen at Londonderry, Victoria Road, in June 1953. The double-decked Craigavon bridge can be seen in the background, spanning the River Foyle – wagons crossing on the lower deck. No 8 was originally No 20 *Raphoe*, introduced in 1908 as Nasmyth, Wilson No 832. She was superheated in 1924 and acquired the new number and the name *Foyle* in 1937. She was scrapped quite early, in 1955.

JM Jarvis/ColourRail

73) No 8 *Foyle* is seen again outside the locomotive shed at Strabane in 1953. To the right, goods wagons and part of the trans-shipment shed can be seen. Railcar trailer No 2 is inside. This shed could take two railcars, normally those used on the early Letterkenny and Stranorlar and Killybegs services.

JM Jarvis/ColourRail

A Class 4 4–6–4 tank locomotive.   **Scale: 4 mm to 1 ft**

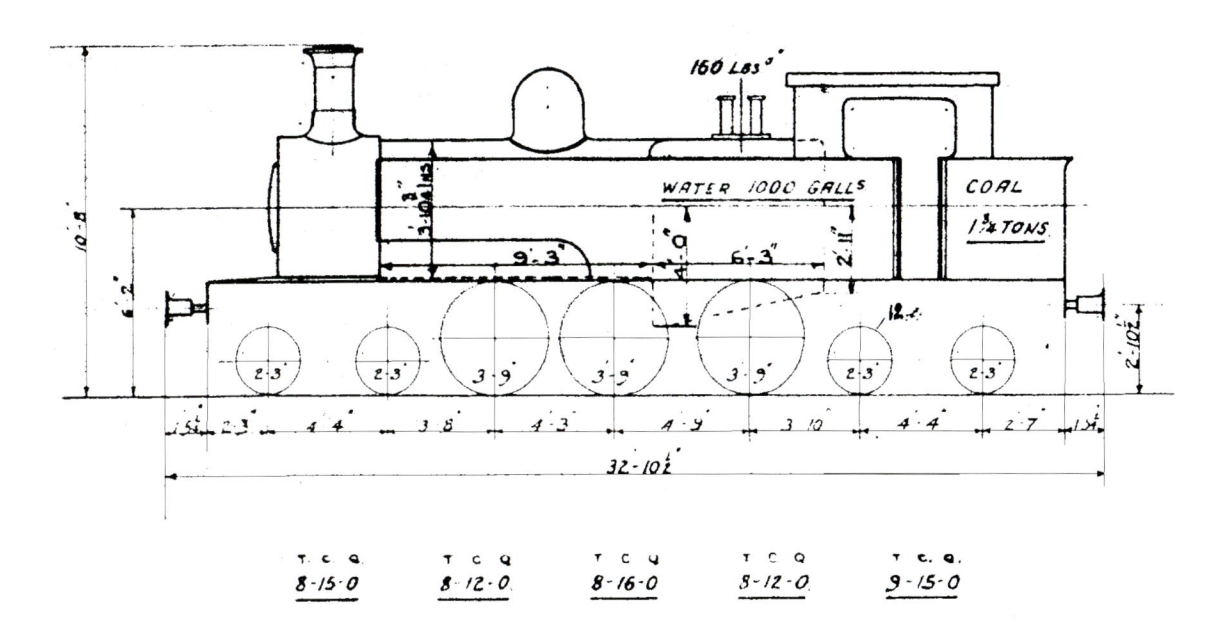

In addition to the Class 5 and 5A locomotives, the CDR has acquired four 'Baltic' 4-6-4 tanks from Nasmyth, Wilson in 1904. One of these, No 11 *Erne*, survived to the end, but her three sisters had been scrapped in the early 1950s. *Erne* started life as No 14, builder's number 699, and was renumbered as No 11 in 1937. Here she is seen shunting a goods at Castlefinn on 9 September 1957. There are sidings over to the left that were used for local traffic and recessing trains awaiting customs clearance. The 'Baltic' tanks weighed 44 tons 10 cwt, carried 1,000 gallons of water, 1¾ tons of coal and had a tractive effort of 14,280 lbs. Driving wheels were 3'9", cylinders 15"x21" and boiler pressure 160 lbs.

R Whitehead/ColourRail

No 11 *Erne* is seen at Stranorlar shed on 22 June 1959. It looks as though she has been dragged out for the photographers as she is not in steam (see the photograph on page 29, top). Francie McMenamin is the driver of No 4 *Meenglas* who has done the pulling. The other 'Baltic' tanks were No 12, *Eske*, re-numbered to No 9 in 1937, builder's number 697, superheated in 1921 and scrapped in 1952; No 13, *Owenea*, re-numbered to No 10 in 1937, builder's number 698, superheated in 1922 and scrapped in 1952; and No 15 *Mourne*, re-numbered to No 12 in 1937, builder's number 700, superheated in 1933 and scrapped after providing spares for the others in 1952. They cost the CDR £2,018 each. *Erne* was sold to Dr Cox, but was stranded at Letterkenny after working the track lifting train. No one realised its importance as the only 3'0" gauge 'Baltic' tank left in the British Isles and she was cut up there, on the failure of the Cox scheme, in 1969.

ColourRail

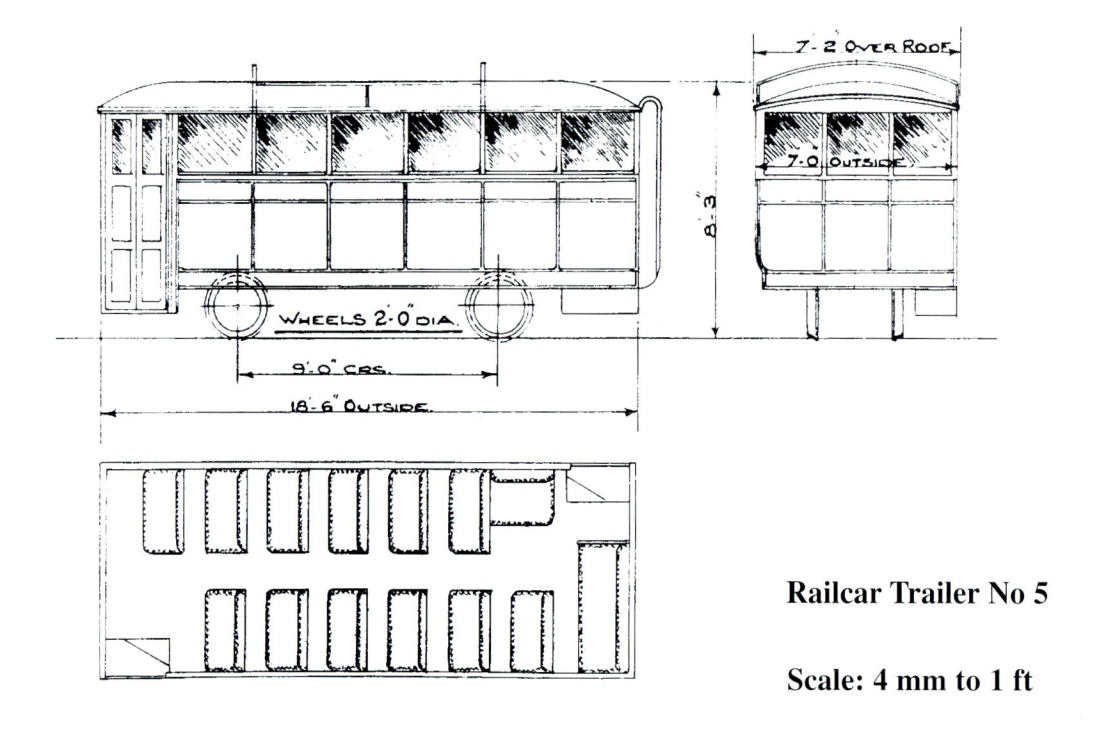

Railcar Trailer No 5

Scale: 4 mm to 1 ft

56

RAILCARS, TRAILERS and PHOENIX

As with many railways, the end of World War One saw many changes and that included a dramatic rise in road transportation of all varieties. Costs increased and, on many railways, ideas were examined to keep these in check, while at the same time increasing patronage. The CDR was the one of the leaders of these endeavours under the inspirational leadership of Henry Forbes, who joined the CDR from the Great Northern in 1916. By 1928 he was Secretary and Manager of the CDR and his influence saw a shift towards the widespread use of railcars.

Railcars could pick up passengers between main stations at halts and many of the latter were opened in the Forbes era. In 1906 the first railcar – really an inspection car – was introduced. It was built by Allday and Onions in Birmingham and had a 10 hp petrol engine. In 1920 it was rebuilt, this time with a much more powerful 26 hp Ford engine and seats for six passengers. It saw service on the Stranorlar to Glenties line and was capable of hauling a 27-seat trailer, proving its worth during the General Strike when coal was in short supply. Happily it now resides in the Ulster Folk and Transport Museum, having originally been sent, in 1956, to the Belfast Transport Museum.

In 1926, two further railcars were acquired from the Derwent Valley Railway in England, operating back to back to avoid turning – these were Nos 2 and 3. They were fitted with Ford 22 hp petrol engines and lasted until 1934. Nos 2 and 3 were then 'replaced' with a 'new' No 2 purchased from Castlederg and Victoria Bridge Tramway and No 3 from the Dublin and Blessington Steam Tramway in 1934. The 'new' No 3 had a Drewry 40 hp petrol engine and carried 40 passengers. It could also, unlike any other CDR railcar, be driven from both ends. It was rebuilt as railcar trailer No 3 in 1944. No 2 was rebuilt with a new 30-seat body and 22 hp engine. It became a trailer in 1944.

Further petrol-driven cars had arrived in 1928. The first, No 4, was motor bus in appearance, and had a 36 hp engine for 22 passengers. This lasted until 1947. Another railcar, No 6, was introduced in 1930 which had 30 seats and was a six-wheeled car with four under the car and the leading two, articulated at the front. It had a Reo 36 hp engine. This too became a trailer in 1945. To make up consecutive numbers, a four-wheeled trailer, No 5, which could carry 29 passengers, was introduced in 1929.

No 7 railcar, introduced in 1931, was diesel powered – the first railcar in the British Isles to be so. With a Gardner 74 hp engine, it could carry 30 passengers and was followed by a sister car No 8. Both lasted until 1949, but in the meantime further cars had been added, with Forbes acquiring two buses to be converted to railcars in 1933. These seated 20, had petrol-driven, Ford, 36 hp engines and were Nos 9 and 10. No 10 was destroyed in a fire at Ballyshannon in 1940 and No 9 was withdrawn in 1949.

The reason for the withdrawal of the earlier cars and the conversion of some to trailers was because of the introduction of the more modern vehicles with power bogies that articulated with the saloon. All the railcars that feature in this book are of this variety, but the trailers are reminders of what had gone before. These articulated cars were all built by Walker Brothers (of Wigan) with Gardner engines, while the saloons were built by the Great Northern's body shops at Dundalk.

No 10 railcar was purchased from the Clogher Valley Railway on its closure in 1941–2. It had been introduced in 1932 and was the first articulated railcar to run in Ireland. Built by Walker Brothers, the railcar had a 74 hp diesel engine and seated 28 passengers. It could also pull trailers and a number of wagons. Numbered 10 by the CDR, it is seen on the turntable at Donegal town on 3 August 1959. Happily the railcar now resides in the Ulster Folk and Transport Museum at Cultra. Note the coupled wheels of the power bogie and the oil tank behind it, built especially for the railcars. The ground signal was interlocked with the point rodding and controlled by the signal cabin. The gentleman walking in the right foreground is Paddy Hannigan.

ES Russell/ColourRail

Two rare photographs show No 12 railcar's motor bogie and cab at Stranorlar detached from the saloon whilst both undergo maintenance. George Brooks, the senior locomotive fitter, walks past as the motor unit prepares to enter the workshops. The saloon would have gone to the carpenter's shops further up the yard. In the background, the saloon of No 10 railcar can be seen.

K Bannister/ColourRail

Another picture, but from a different angle, of No 12's motor bogie at Stranorlar undergoing maintenance. Note the coupled wheels and the workshops behind. The second man in the background is Joe Robinson and the mechanic behind the car on the turntable is Hughie Boner. No 12 was purchased from Walker Brothers in 1934, with a 6L2 Gardner engine. This car also had roller bearings, a four-speed gearbox and was vacuum fitted. It was 12 tons in weight and had a fuel capacity of 40 gallons. It seated 41 passengers and is today stationed at the Foyle Valley Railway in Derry.

K Bannister/ColourRail

No 14 railcar, a red wagon and a grey wagon stand at Strabane. No 14 is just beyond the customs fence – the trestle tables can be seen on the platform for inspection of luggage. In the background are the GNR/CDR exchange sidings and trans-shipment shed (the CDR narrow gauge wagons look nearly as big as the standard gauge GNR ones!). The CDR Derry road runs away on the embankment in the background, swinging right to cross the GNR line that ran to Derry Foyle Road. No 14 was introduced in 1935, a product of Walker Brothers and the GNR. It had a 6L2 Gardner engine (uprated to an 85 hp engine from a 74 hp engine in 1952) and seated 41. Unfortunately it was cut up at Strabane in 1961.

DWK Jones/ColourRail

No 15 railcar was introduced in 1936. It was the first to have a full-width cab. Here it is seen at Donegal town on 19 August 1958 on a service to Killybegs. Another railcar, which looks like No 16 or No 18, is shunting wagons. No 15 had a 74 hp engine and for a time its saloon was swopped with No 14's. Both seated 41 passengers. The remains of this car are now with the County Donegal Restoration Society at Donegal town station.

ColourRail

59

No 19 railcar and No 16 railcar with trailer No 5 stand at Donegal town looking towards Stranorlar on 3 August 1959. These later railcars were much more powerful than those previously mentioned. No 16 was introduced in 1936 with a 102 hp engine. The saloon seated 41. No 5 trailer had been introduced in 1929 and seated 29 passengers. Note the luggage racks on the roofs of the railcars – in reality these were used for bicycles. Working in tandem required a certain art and understanding between motormen to give the passengers a smooth ride, without too much snatching.

ES Russell/ColourRail

Following No 16, a No 17 had been introduced in 1938. This was similar to No 16, but was destroyed in an accident on the Ballyshannon line near Donegal on 29 August 1949 when the driver forgot the train staff and subsequently hit 4-6-4 'Baltic' tank No 10 *Owena*. No 18 railcar was introduced in 1940 and had a 102 hp Gardner engine and, like No 17, 43 seats. No 18's appearance in photographs taken during the period covered by this book is different from the original as it was damaged by fire on 7 November 1949 and had to be re-built. This gave it thicker front window frames and, in Joe Curran's opinion, she "lost some character". She is seen at Donegal town with two grey wagons on 17 March 1959. Happily, she too has survived and is now operational on the Foyle Valley Railway in Derry. Also, she has been restored to her original pre-fire condition.

B Hilton/ColourRail

No 18 railcar's 102 hp Gardner engine and front end are seen in close-up at Donegal on 19 August 1958. The name 'Gardner' can just be made out at the top of the engine itself. The fuel oil filler cap can be seen on the right, together with the top of one of the sandboxes. The CDRJC crest is resplendent on the side of the car and the black lines that separate the cream and crimson livery can be seen – these made all the difference to the smart appearance of the paintwork.

ColourRail

No 19 railcar is seen in 'experimental' livery at Strabane in around 1952. She originally had a full red front but was painted in this condition from 1952 to 1955. She was introduced in January 1950 and was another Walker Brothers/Gardner product, with the coachwork being produced at Dundalk. She carried 41 seated passengers. Not many people really liked the experimental livery and so by approximately 1955 it had changed to a more conventional 'V' shape over the radiator grill. Interestingly, the cover of the 27 June 1954 timetable has a drawing of No 19 mascarading as No 20, complete with Killybegs pier stretching out behind! The trans-shipment shed to the right looks a little battered, but was obviously improved as later pictures show. The grounded coach body on the left was the customs office which provided accommodation for officers. No 19 cost the CDR £8,176 new and on closure was sold to the Isle of Man Railway with her sister, No 20.

R Oakley/ColourRail

61

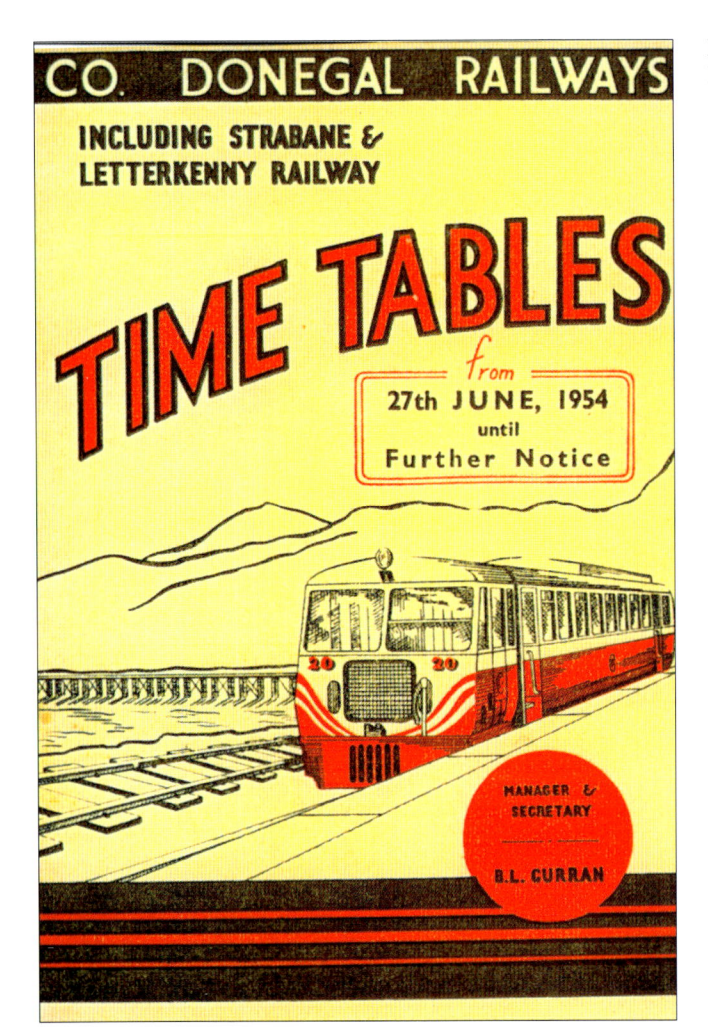

Left: The 1954 timetable showing No 19 in her 1952 livery, but carrying the number 20.

Below: No 20 railcar was a sister car to No 19, but with various detail differences. She is seen carrying her original paint job on the front at Strabane in July 1954. Latterly she carried a wide, and attractive 'V'-type paint job (see photograph on page 14, top). The last of the Walker cars for the CDR, she was delivered in January 1951. Here she is seen with a saloon coach on a Letterkenny service. Some nuns are waiting to board next to the saloon and there are some large hampers to the right – the nearest one with number '7' on it. These were used to carry parcels or other small items. No 20 carried 41 seated passengers and cost the railway £7,885. She was sold, with No 19, to the Isle of Man Railway in 1961. It is interesting to note that there were also four sisters – Nos 3386 to 3389 – of this type of car working on the West Clare Railway. This may have had something to do with the fact that Leo Curran, son of the CDR's General Manager, BL Curran (Joe Curran's brother), was the Mechanical Engineer of the West Clare, and had been impressed by Nos 19 and 20. Unfortunately none of the West Clare cars have survived, although the trailers gave later service on Bord na Mona.

AD Hutchinson/ColourRail

It is 2 August 1959 and No 11 *Phoenix* is seen broadside at Strabane. This curious locomotive amassed 204,577 miles working for the CDR, a line for which it was never intended. The Clogher Valley Railway had been the original recipient of No 11, a steam locomotive with a vertical boiler built by a company called Atkinson, Walker from Preston. They had agreed with the CVR that if the locomotive was not suitable it would be taken back free of charge. Almost immediately Atkinson, Walker went out of business and the locomotive lay unused, having arrived at Aughnacloy in January 1929. It proved seriously underpowered and was an unmitigated failure. Henry Forbes, General Manager of the CDR, was a member of the CVR management committee and realised that it may be possible to convert it to a diesel tractor. It was thus sold to the CDR for 100 guineas, modified with a Gardner diesel engine and was ready to work from the end of 1932. It was named *Phoenix* in acknowledgement of its return. Brilliantly, Forbes sold the boiler from *Phoenix* to a local laundry for £95, thus the locomotive paid for itself!

ES Russell/ColourRail

Phoenix is seen again at Strabane station on 20 August 1958. As well as shunting, *Phoenix* was used for trip working between Lifford and Castlefinn for customs clearance. It occasionally took freights to Stranorlar. GNR railcar A, not a frequent visitor to Strabane before 1957, is seen on the GNR in the background on the standard gauge side. This was built in 1932 and at this time was used on local services between Omagh and Strabane. It was to be preserved but was damaged beyond repair in Derry in 1963. *Phoenix* was preserved and now resides in the Ulster Folk and Transport Museum in Cultra.

ColourRail

Trailer No 2 is pictured at Ballyshannon on 25 May 1957. She was originally a railcar, No 2, and was previously owned by the Castlederg and Victoria Bridge Tramway. There had been another No 2 prior to this, a Derwent Valley car which was scrapped in 1934, the same year as this one arrived. She had a six-cylinder Reo engine installed for use on the CDR, only to be converted to a trailer in 1944, with seats for 30 passengers.

JG Dewing/ColourRail

Trailer No 3 is seen at Stranorlar with No 10 railcar and a coach which are standing on the stub of the Glenties line. Once a 2-2-2-2 railcar, it was originally standard gauge, having been employed on the Dublin and Blessington Steam Tramway. Replacing the original No 3, another Derwent Valley car, it was re-gauged to 3'0" and had a seating capacity of 40 and a 35 hp petrol engine. It could also be driven from both ends without the need for turning. No 3 was rebuilt as a trailer in 1944. It is now preserved at the Ulster Folk and Transport Museum at Cultra.

ColourRail

Trailer No 5 is attached to No 16 railcar and red wagon No 18 at Donegal town on 3 August 1959. She was built in 1929 as a trailer to work with the railcars. At closure she was sold and became a hen house. Thankfully, she is now undergoing restoration at Donegal town. There was also another trailer in service until 1958, No 6, once No 6 railcar, converted in 1945. Red wagon No 18 was an ex-Clogher Valley item, dedicated solely for use with railcars

ES Russell/ColourRail

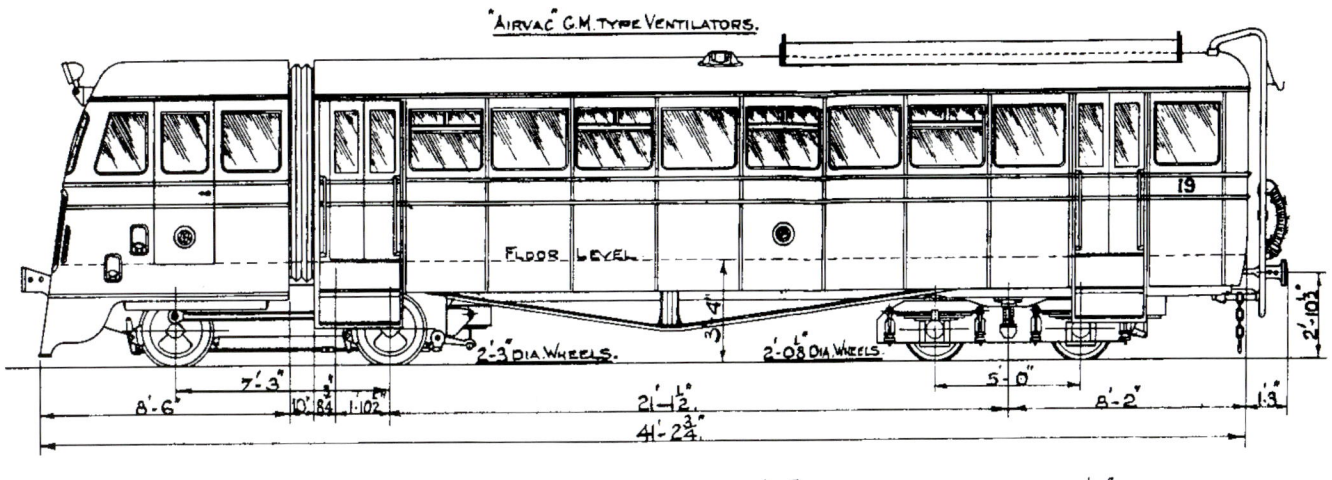

Railcar No 19

Scale: 4 mm to 1 ft

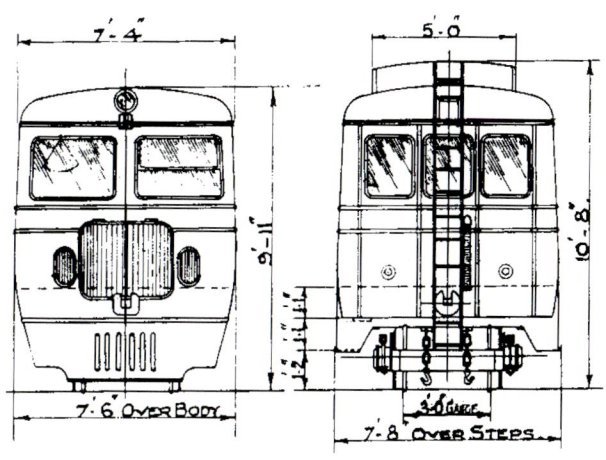

COACHING STOCK

Above: Six-wheel saloon No 1 (the 'Directors' Saloon') is seen at Strabane on 4 August 1958. One of the original West Donegal coaches, she has six wheels, the outside ones having greater lateral movement for cornering. Preserved in the Ulster Folk and Transport Museum, No 1 was built in 1882 by the Railway Carriage and Wagon Company. She was an all-first class vehicle of 28 seats, weighed 9 tons and was 31'0" long. Other vehicles in this series were two composites, five thirds and three passenger vans. No 1 is employed here on a steam-hauled excursion on what seems to be a wet day!

ES Russell/ColourRail

Below: On the same day, we have a rare interior view of saloon No 1 showing the the view to the end doors. This vehicle even had a lavatory. According to Joe Curran, his father 'BL' Curran used to watch this coach go through Stranorlar and ensure that only those who were suitable had permission to travel in it!

ES Russell/ColourRail

Above: Composite coach No 13 is photographed at Ballyshannon on 3 August 1959. Still in use for excursions, the two third class end compartments can be seen, the first class compartment being in the centre. This had six first class seats and each third class compartment carried 22 passengers. She was built by Oldbury in 1893, weighed ten tons and was 31'0" in length.

ES Russell/ColourRail

94) **Below:** A close-up picture of the coat of arms on composite coach No 17 was taken whilst she was on an excursion at Ballyshannon on 2 August 1958. No 17 weighed ten tons and was 31'0" long. She originally had two first class compartments and three third, giving a total of 12 first and 30 third class seats, although all were third by the late 1950s. Another purchase by Dr Cox in 1961, she was built by Oldbury in 1893.

ES Russell/ColourRail

Bogie corridor third No 40 is seen at Ballyshannon on 3 August 1959. She was built by Pickering in 1905, and could seat 60 passengers in two third class compartments. Thirty-six feet long and nine tons in weight, she was purchased by Dr Cox in 1961.

ES Russell/ColourRail

Passenger van No 53 (also purchased by Dr Cox) has been coupled up to a locomotive for a return excursion, again on 3 August 1959 at Ballyshannon. Passenger vans were employed on all CDR freight trains, there being no freight brake vans as all trains were through piped. No 53 was built by Oldbury in 1907 and, in addition to the guard's compartment, had two third class compartments of 20 seats and one first class compartment of six seats.

ES Russell/ColourRail

Composite bogie coach No 56 is seen at Ballyshannon, coupled to No 16 railcar, on 3 August 1959. No 56 was built in 1907, was 36'0" long, and weighed 12 tons. She had two first class compartments that could each seat six passengers and four third class compartments that could carry ten people each – five a side, so it must have been a squeeze! Again, this coach was purchased by Dr Cox in 1961.

ES Russell/ColourRail

68

A view of ex-NCC No 352, CDR No 58 third class coach, built in 1928 for the Ballymena and Larne line boat trains, although No 58's chassis dated from 1879. No 58 is seen at Ballyshannon on 3 August 1959. Originally she had corridor connections, electric lighting and steam heating. She was the shorter of the three purchased by the CDR, being 41'3" long and weighing 13 tons 15 cwt. She had seats for 52 people in two compartments.

ES Russell/ColourRail

All three of the boat train sisters are seen at Ballyshannon beside the up starter on 3 August 1959. The shorter No 58 is to the left, with No 59 in the centre and No 57 to the right, nearest the camera. Both No 57 and No 59 were 50'0" long and weighed 16 tons each. Internally they were different, with No 57 having 54 third class seats in three compartments and No 59 having 54 third class seats in four compartments. All were built in 1928 and were auctioned for scrap in 1961. However, half of one is now a shop at Fintown station.

ES Russell/ColourRail

All scale: 4 mm to 1 ft

Saloon Carriage No 1

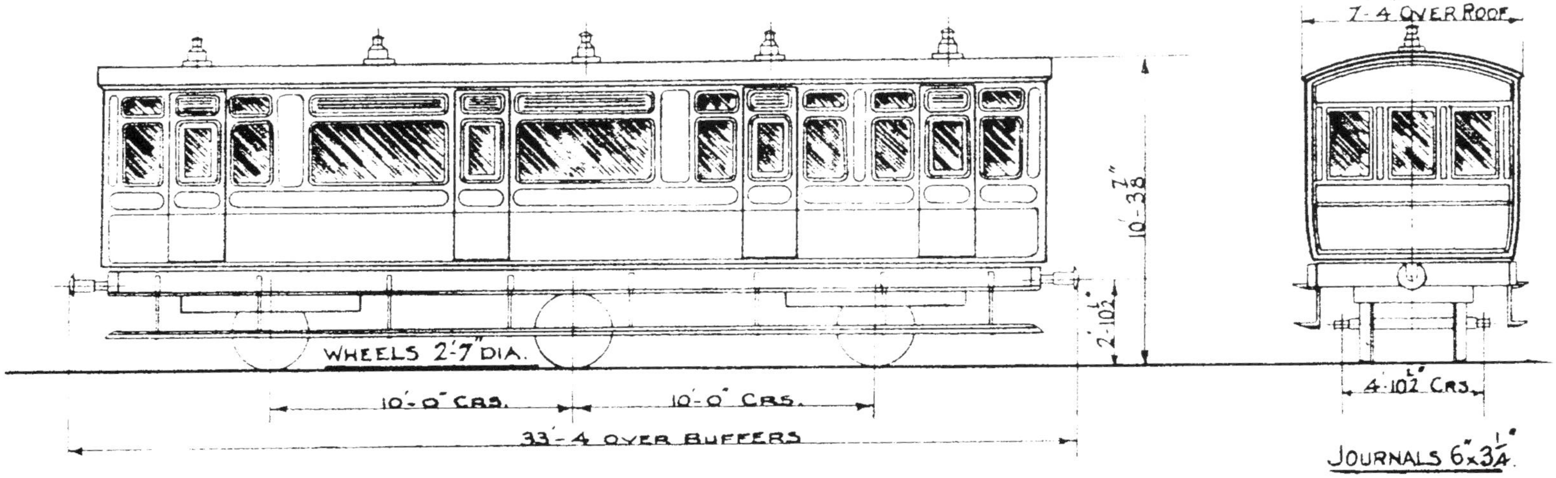

3rd Class Carriages Nos 30, 39, 40

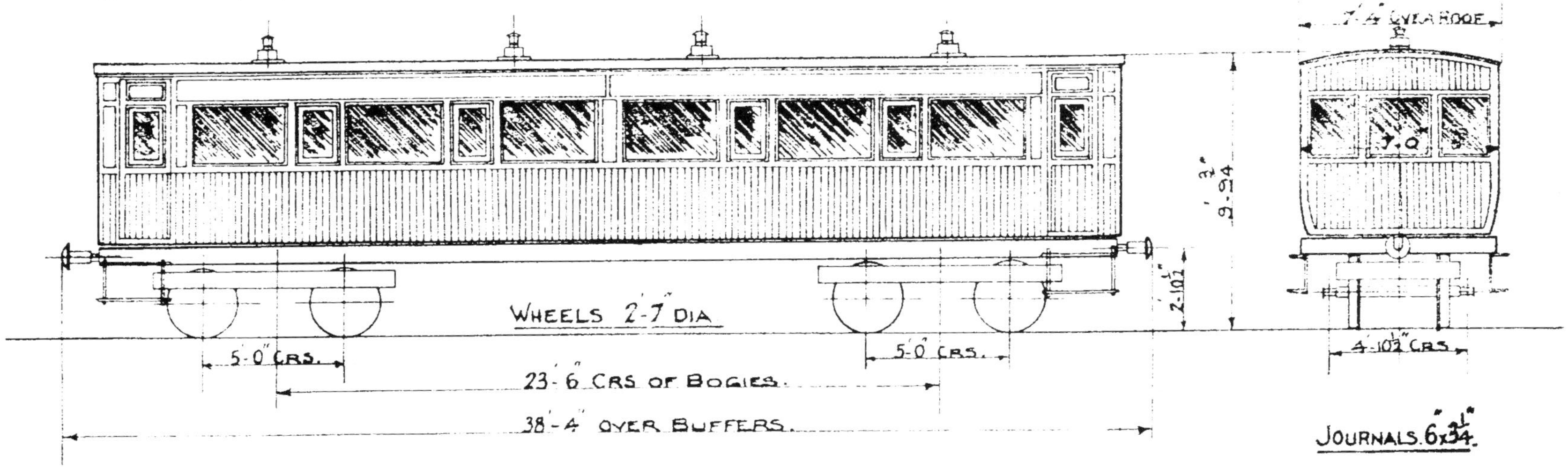

Brake/3rd Carriages Nos 52 – 54

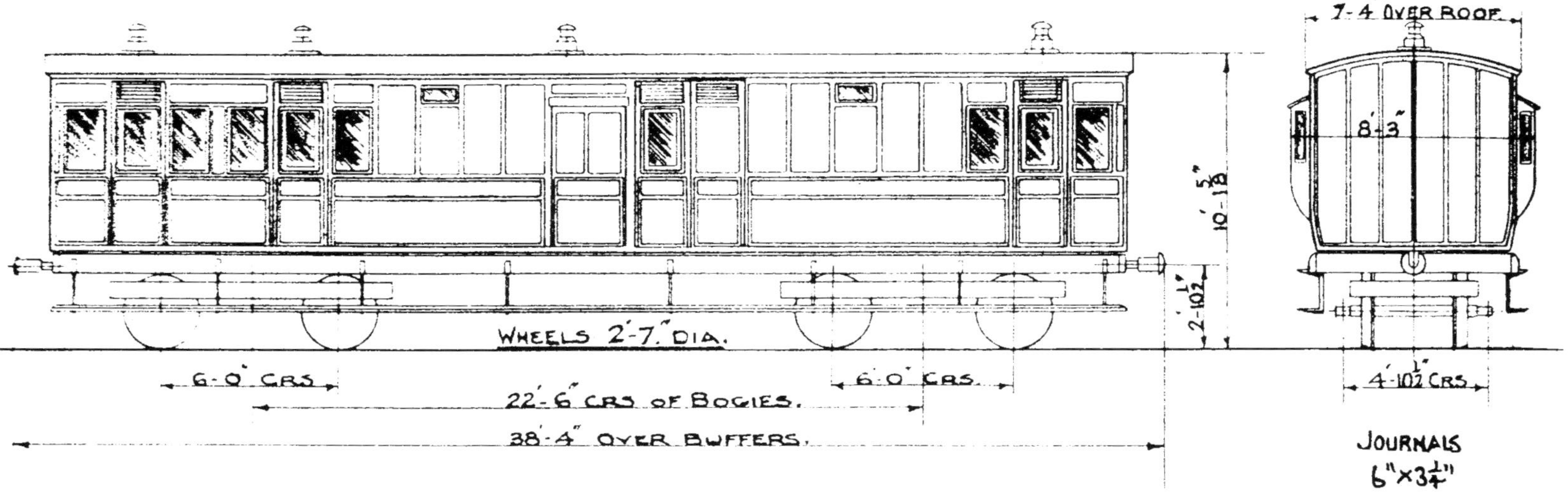

Composite Carriage No 13

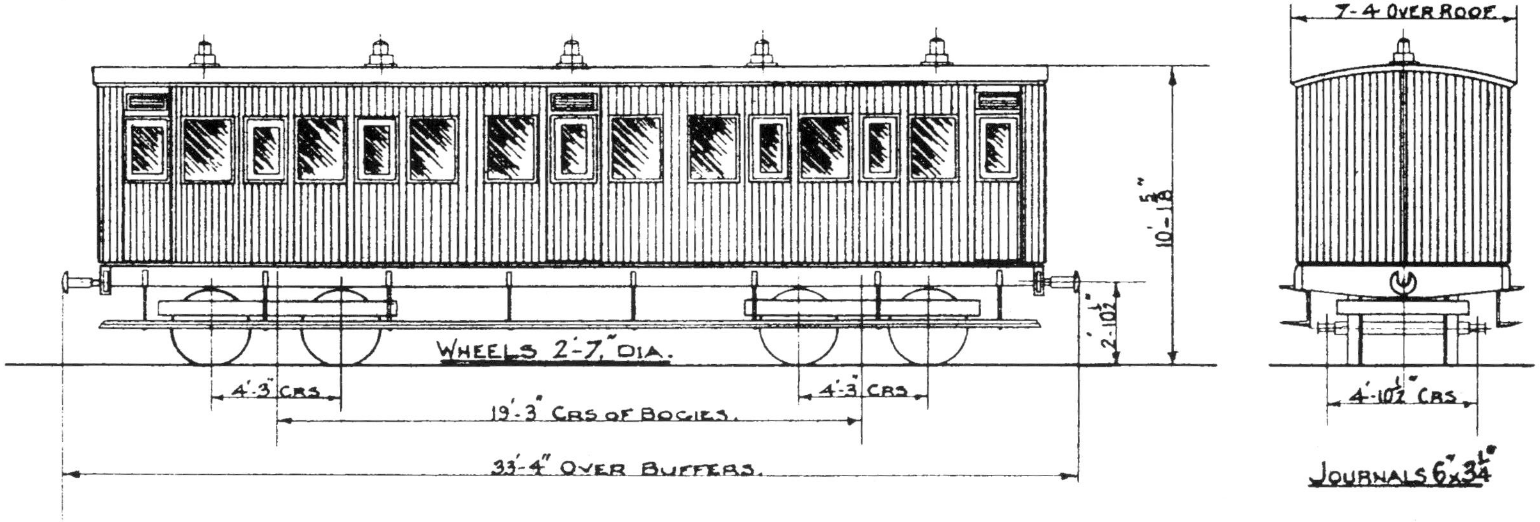

71

RAILCARS ON PASSENGER SERVICES

So what was it like to run the CDR's passenger service – almost exclusively worked by railcars – at this time? Joe Curran has been able to offer an invaluable insight into the profession.

The railcar driver was known as an RCD. One man might be known as RCD Kennedy, another might be known as RCD Herron. It was a very popular position with both staff and passengers and much sought after as an occupation. It had good conditions of service, including a uniform and paid holidays and breaks. All the drivers were of cheerful disposition and this was important as they were in constant contact with the public. Passengers were often welcomed on board, especially as returning émigrés, and some with a shake of the hand!

The RCD was inevitably very busy, with numerous responsibilities – not least the actual skill needed to drive the railcar. This concerned, in the main, the skill to change a gate change (a heavy gear box), a considerable task. Joe Curran was instructed himself on how to do this without jerks and with the job to be completed using the tips of the fingers rather than the force of the body. This was important not only for the comfort of the passengers, but particularly when driving in tandem with another railcar on a larger than average train, in order to minimise jerking. There were four main depots: Stranorlar, Strabane, Killybegs and Letterkenny. Smaller depots were located at Glenties and Ballyshannon. There was no depot at Donegal town as all trains were in transit through here. Railcars did not work to Derry, except on an excursion, so there was no depot there.

Killybegs to Strabane was the longest working – 52½ miles long – and the first railcar from Killybegs was at 07.20. The first duty after breakfast would be to prepare the train. This involved minor maintenance such as checking oil and fuel and inspecting the driving wheel side rods. In addition, before guards were introduced in 1950, the driver would also have a ticket rack and any other details of goods or light goods. He would depart for Donegal and en route pass Dunkineely, Mount Charles and change the ETS (electric train staff) at Inver. Possibly another ten stops would be involved as there were five halts on this line and five authorised railcar stopping places. Before 1950 the driver would have had to issue tickets to joining passengers where there was no station, a duty assumed by the guards from 1950 on. The driver would also supervise collection and deliveries of mails, parcels and newspapers. Arrival at Donegal would be about 08.35. At Donegal town there would be an interchange of passengers with the Ballyshannon line, some more minor goods, such as a bag of flour or even chickens or boxes of other animals. Luggage would be loaded and newspapers unloaded and, more often than not, there would be a red wagon in tow, the loading of which would be supervised by the driver.

The station staff at Donegal town would issue any information required and departure from Donegal would be at 08.42 – only seven minutes. On the Stranorlar road there were three stops, all halts, and at Lough Eske the ETS would be exchanged again. Stranorlar was reached some 45 minutes later and passengers would be exchanged there – picking up passengers from Glenties, until that line closed in 1947.

At Stranorlar another coach, railcar trailer, or even another red wagon would be added for the run to Strabane. Only two halts existed on this stretch, at Town Bridge or Cavan, and a railcar request stop at the County Home, a geriatric hospital. There were two stations on the way to Castlefinn, a major customs station and another crossing point where the ETS was exchanged. Minor customs papers were prepared for the train leaving Éire and it would then arrive at Strabane at 10.50.

At Strabane all passengers and luggage was checked by British customs officers. The railcar would then proceed to the yards where the RCD would turn the railcar, check the interior and then return to Killybegs. At Strabane a red wagon or two would be collected along with a trailer or a coach. As can be seen from the photographs, other wagons were also taken and delivered to points along the Finn Valley. This route was flat and there was no significant loading restriction along the line to Stranorlar. However, going from Stranorlar to Donegal town was a different matter. On the run back, customs completed their entrance requirements at Clady and, as was the case in the opposite direction, the major clearance was done at Castlefinn. The officers got on the train, all passengers were examined off the train, and the RCD would assist in unloading and loading the luggage and also the red wagon. Other halts passed were at Meenglas, originally the home of the founder of the company, Lord Lifford, and then Derg Bridge which handled passengers who were going to cut turf. Then came Lough Eske, a crossing point and ETS point. At Donegal, connection would be made for Ballyshannon, and at Inver a wait may have been experienced to cross another service. The first one in had to recess into the sidings to allow the other to cross (as with Raphoe on the Letterkenny road) and arrival would be in Killybegs at about 15.00. (See the Raphoe diagram on page 20 for an accurate view of this 'loop in the yard'.) After some shunting, the RCD would supervise the unloading of any parcels, mails and newspapers that were brought in and he would then leave the railcar to the new driver to work the mid-afternoon service to Strabane.

Thus the CDR drivers did much more than just drive the railcars – they were ambassadors for the railway and their flexibility allowed the CDR to perform cost effectively for the last three decades of its existence as a rail operator.

The vast majority of timetabled passenger workings in the period covered by this book were operated by the railcars. Steam trains were utilised only in the unlikely event of a railcar failure or on excursion or special workings for such events as bank holidays etc.

A formal passenger timetable was produced and the notice on the facing page appeared inside it under the heading 'General Regulations and Information for Passengers,' issued by the CDR Manager and Secretary BL Curran.

General Regulations and Information for Passengers

The Company hereby gives notice that its Passenger Trains or Rail Cars passing from the Republic of Ireland into Northern Ireland and *vice versa* will stop at the places appointed by the Authorities for the periods specified in the Company's Time Tables, in order that Passengers and their luggage may be examined, and Passengers using the Company's trains or Rail Cars on all such journeys shall be deemed to have made themselves fully acquainted with the Customs and Police Regulations affecting Cross-Border travel.

In the event of it being found impossible to have the luggage, or any portion thereof, belonging to any passenger, examined, or for the passengers to satisfy both of these authorities within the specified period, **the Train or Rail Car will not be delayed.** Any unexamined luggage will be taken out and forwarded to destination as soon as possible thereafter, and the company shall not be liable for any loss, damage, or expenses which the passenger owning such luggage may sustain by reason of any such delay, or as a result of any personal detention by any of these Authorities.

Despatch of Trains or Rail Cars at Junction Stations. The Company reserves the right to despatch Trains or Rail Cars from Junction Stations before the arrival of other Trains or Rail Cars shown in the Company's Time Table as connecting Trains or Rail Cars, should such other Trains or Rail Cars be running late.

Time Tables. The Company does not undertake that the Services shall start or arrive at the time specified in the Time Tables, nor will it be accountable for any loss, inconvenience or injury, which may arise from delay or detention unless upon proof that such loss, inconvenience, injury, delay or detention arose in consequence of the wilful misconduct of the Company's servants.

Passengers entering wrong Train. The Company does not accept the responsibility of seeing that Passengers enter the right Train or Rail Car, and will not accept any liability for any loss occasioned to any person entering the wrong Train or Rail Car.

B. L. CURRAN,

Manager and Secretary.

Summary of Principal Through Services
Strabane — Donegal — Killybegs

		a.m.	a.m.	a.m.	p.m.	p.m.	p.m.	p.m. S.O.	p.m.
STRABANE	dep.	7.45	9.50	11.20	2.40	4.50	6.10	6.10	8. 0
STRANORLAR	arr.	8.31	10.40	12.12	3.32	5.33	6.50	6.50	8.40
DONEGAL	,,	9.24	—	1. 9	4.30	6.44	—	7.51	—
INVER	,,	9.58	—	2. 3	5.25	7.16	—	8.25	—
KILLYBEGS	,,	10.35	—	2.35	6. 1	7.50	—	9. 0	—

		a.m.	a.m.	a.m.	a.m.	p.m.	p.m.	p.m.	p.m. S.O
KILLYBEGS	dep.	—	—	7.45	9.27	—	12.30	3.50	6.35
INVER	,,	—	—	8.22	10. 1	—	1. 5	4.26	7.18
DONEGAL	,,	—	—	8.55	10.34	—	1.42	5. 0	7.58
STRANORLAR	,,	6.45	8.45	9.55	11.29	1.20	2.40	6. 5	8.45
STRABANE	arr.	7.28	9.30	10.40	12.12	2. 2	3.25	6.50	—

S.O.— SATURDAYS ONLY.

No 14 railcar is waiting at Strabane with three red wagons as she prepares to leave for Letterkenny on 20 August 1959. The Letterkenny road forked sharply west at Strabane and crossed the River Foyle on a 293 feet long girder bridge. Next came Lifford and the Irish Republic customs check. Ballindrait was then passed, followed by a number of crossings or 'gates' known by the name of the gate keeper. Thus, O'Brien, Devenny and Donnelly preceded Coolaghy Halt, followed by Raphoe. Some of these were official railcar stops, but railcars would in fact stop at all of these 'gates' if required.

ColourRail

No 14 railcar, a coach (probably No 30 which was fitted with roller bearings and bucket seats for use with railcars) and two red wagons are seen at Raphoe on 12 May 1959. These station buildings are still extant today.

JG Dewing/ColourRail

No 16 railcar is seen cooling off at Letterkenny, having arrived on a service from Strabane. From Raphoe, gates would have been crossed at Cairns, Chambers, and Linney's before Convoy was reached. Then followed gates at Mulrine, Gillen and Ayton's before Cornagillagh Halt was passed. The route continued with Glenmaquin, followed by more gates at Doherty, Parke, Maguire, Martin, Killen's, and Baird's. The date is 31 May 1957. The next task would be to turn the railcar for the run back to Strabane. Note the interlocked ground signal and catch point which will let No 16 out of the siding road.

FW Shuttleworth/ColourRail

No 10 railcar, with trailer No 2, has just turned and is pulling into Strabane station to work a service to Stranorlar and Killybegs on 2 August 1958. There were seven services from Strabane to Stranorlar on weekdays, four of these going through to Killybegs, with an extra evening working on Saturdays from Stranorlar to Strabane. The ground signal which guards the entrance to the main line from the shed is 'off' to allow access to the platform roads. The Derry line is in the foreground, now having closed beyond station limits and being limited to shunting moves.

ES Russell/ColourRail

75

No 12 railcar stands at Platform 3 at Strabane by the customs barrier on 19 March 1956. The sign still points the way for Glenties, although this was now a bus service that ran three times a day to and from Strabane. Pat Madden stands on the left, dressed in full uniform, the senior and most respected CDR/GNR man at Strabane station. He carried out ticket checks both on and off the trains. No 12 has a service for Stranorlar and Killybegs.

ES Russell/ColourRail

Portnoo — Glenties — Dungloe — Dublin — Belfast

			a.m.	p.m.	p.m.
PORTNOO	(Road)	dep.	8.0	12.30	4.5
DUNGLOE	(Road)	,,	—	12.0	—
GLENTIES	(Road)	,,	8.30	1.0	4.35
STRANORLAR	(Rail)	,,	9.55	2.40	6.5
BELFAST	(Rail)	arr.	3.55	7.0	10.0
DUBLIN	(Rail)	,,	6.5	9.25	—
			a.m.	a.m.	p.m.
DUBLIN	(Rail)	dep.	—	9.0	—
BELFAST	(Rail)	,,	8.25	11.15	2.10
STRANORLAR	(Road)	,,	12.20	3.50	7.0
GLENTIES	(Road)	arr.	1.40	5.10	8.20
DUNGLOE	(Road)	,,	6.5	6.5	9.15A
PORTNOO	(Road)	,,	2.10	5.40	8.50

A.— SATURDAYS ONLY.

Stranorlar—Glenties—Portnoo Route

WEEK-DAYS

		a.m.	p.m.	p.m.	p.m.
STRANORLAR (C.D.R.)	dep.	8.40	12.20	3.50	7.0
BROCKAGH	,,	9.10	12.48	4.18	7.28
FINTOWN P.O.	,,	9.35	1.12	4.42	7.52
GLENTIES	,,	10.10	1.40	5.10	8.20
MAAS HOTEL (Molloy's)	,,	10.25	1.55	5.25	8.35
PORTNOO	arr.	10.40	2.10	5.40	8.50

		a.m.	p.m.	p.m.	p.m.
PORTNOO	dep.	8.0	12.30	—	4.5
MAAS HOTEL (Molloy's)	,,	8.15	12.45	—	4.20
GLENTIES	,,	8.30	1.0	2.35	4.35
FINTOWN P.O.	,,	8.57	1.27	3.2	5.2
BROCKAGH	,,	9.20	1.50	3.25	5.25
STRANORLAR (C.D.R.)	arr.	9.50	2.20	3.55	5.55

No 16 railcar, trailer No 2 and two red wagons pause at Castlefin for a customs check. The trestle tables can be seen on the platform and luggage can be seen being inspected. The procedure involved was for the train to stop at the platform before it reached the tables. Everyone would get out with their luggage (which would have been unloaded from the red wagon by railway staff) and go through clearance at the tables. The train itself would then be inspected and after that it would draw forward, past the tables and, when people were fully checked, they could get back on and the journey continue.

RC Ludgate/ColourRail

No 12 railcar, with two wagons in tow, gets away from Stranorlar on 13 September 1957 on the 07.45 from Killybegs to Strabane. The time is 09.55. To the right is passenger van No 41 which, in addition to the guard, carried 20 third class passengers.

C Hogg/ColourRail

77

No 10 railcar, with two wagons, waits to leave Stranorlar with a service for Donegal. This would take the train through the famous Barnesmore Gap and past the spectacular Lough Mourne on the former West Donegal road – the original 3'0" gauge part of the railway. When this had been a mixed gauge station, the Finn Valley line had come in to the left and terminated by the station buildings. The narrow gauge West Donegal had had its platform roughly where No 10 is seen here, on the other side of an island platform from the Finn Valley.

K Cooper/ColourRail

The first main feature on the Donegal road was the bridge over the River Finn and No 16 railcar, trailer 5 and red wagon No 18 cross this bridge as they enter Stranorlar from Donegal on 2 August 1959. Note the white plate on the rear of the wagon denoting the end of the train.

ES Russell/ColourRail

78

This was the real 'Wee Donegal'! From Stranorlar, the line climbed through Meenglas at 1:59 for a mile, then 1:50 for a mile and then three miles at 1:60 through the summit at 592 feet at Derg Bridge. No 10 railcar, trailer No 5 and a wagon pass through the spectacular scenery of the Barnesmore Gap on the descent from the summit to Lough Eske on 19 May 1956.

ES Russell/ColourRail

A little later, No 10 railcar, trailer 5 and a wagon arrive at Lough Eske with the Stranorlar service on 19 May 1956. From Lough Eske the line descended through Clar Bridge to Donegal town. Note the passing loop here, the station being to the right of the photographer on single track.

ES Russell/ColourRail

The driver of No 10 railcar and trailer No 2 receives the train staff for the road to Stranorlar as she prepares to leave with a service from Donegal town. The man with his hand on the cab is Willie Hegarty, the signalman at Donegal town. RCD Christie Kennedy is the gentleman in the coat walking towards the photographer. The train to his left has just come in from Strabane and the mails are being unloaded from the red wagon. The date is 22 May 1958.

ES Russell/ColourRail

No 18 railcar, with Joe Thompson doing the driving, arrives at Donegal town from Ballyshannon on 3 August 1959. A coach makes up the rest of the train. Note the two small side lights on the front of the railcar – this was the only car to carry such lights, these having been fitted whilst the railcar was re-built at Dundalk; other cars made do with just the powerful head lamp. The fine array of signals can be seen in the background. No 19 railcar waits to leave for Strabane and No 10 railcar is on the turntable behind. Does anyone know what happened to the film being taken by the gentleman in the red shirt who is standing by the signal?

ES Russell/ColourRail

The end of the line was at Killybegs. No 19 railcar stands with a grey wagon, with its crew posing for the camera. The driver, seen on the left is Cahal Kennedy and the guard is Tommy Kenny. Cahal Kennedy's brother Frank Kennedy was the stationmaster at Killybegs. Tommy Kenny is holding his rack of tickets and behind the scene is the turntable. No 19 was later to leave with a train for Donegal, Stranorlar and Strabane on 20 May 1957.

FW Shuttleworth/ColourRail

A good close–up is had of the train shed on 11 May 1959 as No 12 railcar and a red wagon wait for departure time at Killybegs. Cahal Kennedy is driving once more on this Strabane service. The loading bank and goods store are seen behind the train. The centre line to the left leads to the pier which is further over to the left of the photograph, crossing over another siding by means of a small diamond crossing (see page 38 for a track plan).

JG Dewing/ColourRail

81

Donegal — Ballyshannon

		a.m.	p.m.	p.m.	p.m.	Su.O. p.m.
DONEGAL	dep.	9.29	1.35	6.10	8. 5	—
ROSSNOWLAGH	arr.	10. 1	2.11	6.43	8.34	12. 0
BALLYSHANNON	arr.	10.19	2.25	6.58	8.52	12.20

		a.m.	Noon	p.m.	p.m.	Su.O. a.m.
BALLYSHANNON	dep.	8. 0	12. 0	4. 0	7.10	10.30
ROSSNOWLAGH	,,	8.18	12.18	4.18	7.25	10.50
DONEGAL	arr.	8.50	12.55	4.50	7.58	—

Su.O.— Sundays Only.

Strabane — Letterkenny

		a.m.	a.m	p.m.	p.m.	p.m.	Su.O. p.m.
STRABANE	dep.	8.10	11.20	2.35	5.35	8.10	11.55
LETTERKENNY	arr.	9.18	12.32	3.52	6.47	9.15	1.20

		a.m.	a.m.	p.m.	p.m.	p.m.	p.m.
LETTERKENNY	dep.	8. 0	11.15	2.35	5.30	6.57	9.30
STRABANE	arr.	9.10	12.25	3.48	6.36	8. 0	10.35

Su.O — Sundays Only.

No 18 railcar is pictured on arrival at Ballyshannon on 23 June 1959. A grey wagon is in tow and mail is about to be loaded for the return trip. The common theme that runs through all these photographs of railcars on passenger services is their versatility: not only did they carry passengers but they also had room for luggage, mails and parcels in their red wagons; they could pull a couple of freight wagons; they could shunt; and they could do all of this at a fraction of the cost of steam operation.

ColourRail

82

STEAM HAULED PASSENGER SERVICES

No 1 *Alice* waits to leave Londonderry, Victoria Road, with a Strabane service in October 1953. The line from Derry to Strabane was operated by the Ulster Transport Authority under contract to the CDR. The UTA had acquired the line from the LMS in 1948 and it was always operated by steam traction. This was because railcars were best employed on the CDR's own services, as they were cheaper to run than steam. Also, the CDR were able to add wagons of coal for locos, oil for the railcars and other freight wagons to these trains at no extra cost. In this photograph some of the CDR's oil tankers, used to convey oil for the fishing fleet at Killybegs and for its own railcars, can be seen, as well as open wagon No 141 and wagon No 36, both in the goods dock. The white spot on No 36 indicates that the top sides can be dropped to make it into a cattle wagon, and the white 'X' further down means that it is not train braked, but through piped, having been re-built at Dundalk in 1946–7. There were three trains per day on the line, departing Strabane at 09.40 am, 12.30 pm and 3.30 pm, and running from Derry at 06.50 am, 2.00 pm and 4.25 pm.

WE Robertson/ColourRail

No 4 *Meenglas* is seen at Castlefin on 22 June 1959. She is hauling a goods service with a passenger coach included in the formation for an enthusiasts' visit. She has stopped for customs clearance and the enthusiasts are taking time to look around. A wagon is in the platform to the right for unloading. A large box that was used to carry Jacob's biscuits is seen on the right, awaiting loading for return.

ColourRail

83

Excursions

Excursions provided important income for the CDR and was another illustration of how the railway served the needs of the local community and those who travelled to Donegal from further afield. In 1955 12,000 passengers travelled on CDR excursions. Many of the trains were 'hardy annuals' organised by the CDR rather than private individuals and catered for bank holidays such as the first Monday in August, Easter Monday, Whitsun, and for the Killybegs Regatta at the harbour. In addition, there were semi-religious festivals such as the Orange demonstration in Rossnowlagh, traditionally held on the first Saturday in July when there was a parade to the beach, bands travelling from Counties Cavan, Sligo and Monaghan as well as Donegal. Another festival was that of 15 August which could rotate between say Ballyshannon, Letterkenny and then Stranorlar or Killybegs. They were all very well patronised and exciting for those taking part.

Sunday excursions were run to Rossnowlagh, often with two trains of 12 coaches running from Strabane and Stranorlar on the same day. Some passengers alighted at Rossnowlagh, others going on to Ballyshannon for Bundoran where the GNR buses met the CDR trains. The churches also used the CDR for Sunday school trips to Portrush, the train taking them as far as Derry, from where they would catch the NCC service to Portrush, returning late in the evening.

All excursions were family events: children went to the seaside with their parents; teenagers and courting couples went to Rossnowlagh. Grandparents would also accompany the family – often grannie would go to the beach and help mind the children while grandpa headed off to one of the local hostelries! The outward journey was very exciting and, as can be seen from the photographs, many travellers leant out of the windows. The return journeys were more subdued as people were tired, but comments such as 'see you next year' were often heard.

The most interesting excursion was 'The Hills of Donegal' which ran most summer Sundays. It left Belfast at approximately 08.30 and travelled down to Strabane, arriving at 11.00. The CDR would provide two railcars and a coach or trailers and a fast run was had to Donegal town, non-stop through Stranorlar. The hotels in Donegal town would receive advance notice of the imminent arrival by telephone. The patrons would walk to the hotels, have a look at Donegal town and then catch the now turned railcars for the run to Ballyshannon. At Ballyshannon, a GNR bus took them to Bundoran where they stayed from three o' clock to approximately seven o'clock. From there they would catch a train back to Belfast – the same train that had deposited them at Strabane earlier that day. This had run back through Omagh and Bundoran Junction.

No 5 *Drumboe* has a long train at Stranorlar for Ballyshannon on 4 August 1958. This would have been an excursion, the fourth coach from the camera being Directors' Saloon No 1. There were many specials and excursions run on the CDR which meant that much steam rolling stock lived on. As well as bank holiday excursions, there were trains to and from Killybegs Regatta and Sports, excursions that provided connections for Dublin and Belfast, and a number of trains associated with various demonstrations such as the Apprentice Boys' Relief of Derry parade, as well as specials for the Ancient Order of Hibernians. There was also another special working, 'The Hills of Donegal', which took passengers on a round trip to Ballyshannon utilising the CDR and the GN branch to Bundoran, this line also having a station in Ballyshannon.

ES Russell/ColourRail

A year later and No 4 *Meenglas* waits at Stranorlar with another train for Ballyshannon on August bank holiday Monday, 3 August 1959.
ES Russell/ColourRail

Shortly afterwards, No 4 *Meenglas* is seen leaving Stranorlar and crossing the Finn on its way to Ballyshannon. The train is only six coaches long, not too taxing a load for a steam locomotive of this quality on this steeply graded section. The date is 3 August 1959.
ES Russell/ColourRail

C.D.R.

SUNDAY AFTERNOON EXCURSIONS
TO
ROSSNOWLAGH

ON THE FOLLOWING DATES :—

JUNE:— 27th

JULY:— 4th, 11th, 18th and 25th

AUGUST:— 1st, 8th, 15th, 22nd and 29th

SEPTEMBER:— 5th

In connection with above, the following Special Trains will run :—

		p.m.	p.m.	Return Fare
STRABANE	dep.		1.30	5/6
CLADY	,,		1.40	5/0
CASTLEFIN	,,		1.50	4/6
LISCOOLY	,,		1.55	4/6
KILLYGORDON	,,		2. 5	4/0
STRANORLAR	,,		2.13	3/6
DONEGAL	,,	1.50	3.10	2/5
ROSSNOWLAGH	arr.	2.20	3.40	—

TICKETS VALID DAY OF ISSUE ONLY

RETURN TRAIN LEAVES ROSSNOWLAGH AT 8 p.m.

B. L. CURRAN,
Manager and Secretary.

No 4 *Meenglas* is seen again, this time at Lough Mourne on 3 August 1959. The passengers look in good heart on this bank holiday Monday as they head off to Ballyshannon. Note the lack of trees in this area. *ES Russell/ColourRail*

Another excursion ran on the same day, this time with No 2 *Blanche* in charge. Here she is seen at Lough Mourne with more happy revellers for Ballyshannon. This time a much heavier train is under tow with no fewer than nine coaches being hauled over the summit at Derg Bridge. Note the extra width of the Ballycastle coaches, third, sixth and seventh in the train. Despite this being the last season of excursions on the railway, they were still extremely popular – there were no signs of decline at all, which was much the same for general passengers and freight.

ES Russell/ColourRail

No 4 *Meenglas* returns later in the day through Derg Bridge on 3 August 1959. No fewer than eleven coaches seem to be on this one and all three Ballycastle coaches are visible. The locomotive is now blowing off as she had obviously been well fired up for the run up from Donegal town through the Barnesmore Gap. Now it is downhill to Stranorlar.
ES Russell/ColourRail

A complete excursion train is viewed, but this time one year earlier, on 4 August 1958. This is another bank holiday Monday excursion from Strabane to Ballyshannon, loading 11 coaches, viewed passing through the Barnesmore Gap hauled by No 2 *Blanche*.
ES Russell/ColourRail

No 4 *Meenglas* with '11 on' is seen on 3 August 1959 storming up the Barnesmore Gap with her return excursion. The remoteness here is well illustrated, with the train clinging to the side of the Blue Stack Mountains. Note also the telegraph poles, vital in transporting all the telecommunications services that the railway required to keep it running. This would not only allow voice telephony between stations and signal cabins, but also operated the various block sections.

ES Russell/ColourRail

No 2 *Blanche* is seen on 3 August 1959 at Barnesmore station with her Strabane to Ballyshannon excursion of ten coaches. The Ballycastle coaches are third, sixth and seventh.

ES Russell/ColourRail

No 4 *Meenglas* is seen at Lough Eske with her Strabane to Ballyshannon excursion on 3 August 1959. She is pulling out of the loop where Strabane trains could be crossed if necessary. No 4 has a good head of steam on and is blowing off, relaxing a bit as she descends to Donegal after the long climb from Stranorlar.

ES Russell/ColourRail

No 4 *Meenglas* pauses at Lough Eske on 22 June 1959. Jim McMenamin is checking the side rod on the locomotive to ensure she is not running hot. The station building still stands at Lough Eske, but unfortunately the N15 main road passes to the right of it. – not as classy as the 'Wee Donegal'! Of course, Lough Eske was the original terminus of the West Donegal Railway, named Druminin. This was because there was insufficient capital to take the line to Donegal town, so a horse-drawn road service was provided from here to and from Donegal town from its opening on 25 April 1882. Eventually money was raised to get the line to Donegal town, but not until 16 September 1889. The station at Donegal town was built by a separate company, the Donegal Railway Station Company, and this was leased to the West Donegal for £200 per annum! The lamp on the station – which does not look to be in working order – is probably a throwback to earlier years when the station was the terminus.

ColourRail

No 2 *Blanche* arrives at Donegal town with her special for Ballyshannon from Strabane on 3 August 1959. Jim McKenna can be seen on the footplate. In the background the signal is off for an arrival from Stranorlar, the other gantry controlling the Ballyshannon line. The next task will be to run round the train so it can depart for Ballyshannon.
ES Russell/ColourRail

After the 'hard slog' over the Blue Stack Mountains to Donegal, it is time for *Blanche* to top up her tanks for the run to Ballyshannon. She is seen with 'the bag in' at Donegal water column, with Jim McKenna officiating. It looks as though they have quickly cleaned the fire as some burning ash can be seen on the ground near the cab door. Jim McKenna had accumulated 44 years of service when the line closed – a remarkable achievement, but in the railway industry this sort of loyalty is not uncommon. The date is again 3 August 1959.
ES Russell/Colour Rail

90

A year earlier No 2 *Blanche* leaves Donegal town with an excursion for Ballyshannon on 4 August 1958. The locomotive inspector Paddy McBride is in the brown coat climbing onto the engine. The brown inspector's coat and hat seemed to be standard dress for inspectors wherever one went! Some serious photography takes place on the left!
ES Russell/ColourRail

Ballyshannon yard is seen with stabled excursion stock and loco No 5 *Drumboe* on 4 August 1958. As can be seen, enthusiasts have realised these excursions were running and have (thankfully for this book) turned up to photograph them. To the left of the locomotive is the railcar shed and the coaches are stabled in the cattle dock. The water tower is to the right and behind that is the turn table.
ES Russell/ColourRail

91

On the same day, No 2 *Blanche* arrives at Ballyshannon on another special. No 5 *Drumboe* and her train can be seen to the right. That tripod is in action again!

ES Russell/ColourRail

One year later (with better weather), on 3 August 1959, No 2 *Blanche* has arrived at Ballyshannon with another excursion. One of the many enthusiasts who were filming that weekend talks to locomotive inspector Paddy McBride (in the soft hat). The gentleman to his right is Paddy Gallagher who was the youngest driver on the CDR, appointed at the age of 36.

ES Russell/ColourRail

92

County Donegal Railways Joint Committee

BANK HOLIDAY
Monday 3rd August, 1959

SPECIAL EXCURSION

to
Rossnowlagh Ballyshannon, and Killybegs

In connection with above, Cheap Excursion Tickets (valid day of issue only) will be issued for the undermentioned Trains from :—

RETURN FARES

		a.m.	Noon	To Rossnowlagh	To Ballyshannon and Killybegs
STRANORLAR	dep.	9.30	—	5/3d.	6/3d.
DONEGAL	dep.	10.49	12. 5	2/10d.	4/3d.
ROSSNOWLAGH	arr.	11.35	12.55	—	—
BALLYSHANNON	arr.	12. 0	1.20	—	—
KILLYBEGS	arr.	12.20	—	—	—

RETURN SERVICE will LEAVE
- Killybegs at 6-30 p.m.
- Ballyshannon at 8- 0 p.m.
- Rossnowlagh at 8-25 p.m.

Serving above Stations only

Bundoran FREQUENT OMNIBUS SERVICES TO AND FROM BUNDORAN WILL CONNECT WITH ABOVE TRAINS AT BALLYSHANNON STATION.

Excursion Tickets will not be issued for, and accommodation will be strictly limited on, subsequent Trains Above Specials will run non-stop from Stranorlar to Donegal and Donegal to Rossnowlagh.

B. L. Curran,
MANAGER AND SECRETARY.

STRANORLAR, 3-7-'59.

"DEMOCRAT," BALLYSHANNON

STEAM HAULED FREIGHT SERVICES

The CDR freight services always seemed to be busy. Booked freights ran daily or on specific days of the week or month, depending on local circumstances such as market days. Specials would be run on an 'as required' basis. Decline in freight forwardings was evident from the 1930s when over 90,000 tons of traffic was carried per annum. By the 1950s only 30,000 tons a year was using the CDR, the majority of which was livestock. This livestock traffic declined significantly by closure but the CDR's road services picked up most of the business, which was almost exclusively moving animals out of Donegal. The majority of other freight flowed into Donegal from outside, but the railway was the main carrier of coal from Derry and Killybegs. Usually an attempt was made to get a back load for the wagon, but in the case of coal or oil this was not possible unless, in the former case, building materials such as wood or permanent way materials could be carried. Forwardings to and from places were varied, but freight forwardings and receipts were based on the following traffic at these stations (livestock was cattle, horses and sheep; general merchandise mainly potatoes and grain):

Derry
- Coal forwardings
- Oil forwardings for railway use and Killybegs for the fishing fleet
- Inwards livestock from various markets
- Inwards potatoes, beer and minerals and general merchandise
- Inwards wool for export from Donegal

Strabane
- Customs clearance activities
- Connection with CDR road services
- Exchange sidings with the Great Northern for import/export
- Forwarding and receipt of beer and minerals, return of empties in crates
- Receipt of livestock inwards for market or onwards shipping
- Forwarding of farm machinery
- Forwarding and receipt of general merchandise
- Forwarding and receipt of newspapers, mails and parcels traffic
- Receipt of fuel oil for railcars and coal for merchants and railway use

Lifford
- Customs clearance post
- Forwarding and receipt of Post Office mails
- Forwarding and receipt of general merchandise
- Receipt of agricultural products
- Receipt of coal

Convoy
- Receipt of coal for CW Co
- Forwarding of woollen products from Convoy Woollen Mills
- Receipt of agricultural machinery and other materials
- Forwarding and receipt of general merchandise
- Forwarding of livestock

Raphoe
- Forwarding and receipt of livestock – there was a fair here
- Receipt of agricultural machinery and other materials
- Forwarding and receipt of general merchandise
- Receipt of coal

Letterkenny
- Connection with CDR road services
- Fowarding and receipt of livestock – notably the Oldtown cattle fair
- Forwarding and receipt of general merchandise
- Forwarding and receipt of letter mails, parcels and newspapers
- Receipt of agricultural machinery
- Receipt of beers and other minerals – forwarding of the empties
- Receipt of fuel oil for railcars and coal for merchants and railway use

Stranorlar
- Connection with CDR road services
- Fowarding and receipt of livestock
- Receipt of fuel oil for railcars and coal for merchants and railway use
- Forwarding and receipt of general merchandise
- Forwarding and receipt of letter mails, parcels and the carriage of newspapers was free to Eason's bookstall on the station!
- Receipt of agricultural machinery
- Receipt of beers and other minerals – forwarding of the empties
- Receipt of engineering materials and railway equipment

Castlefinn
- Customs clearance post
- Receipt of beers and minerals – forwarding of the empties
- Forwarding of livestock
- Forwarding and receipt of general merchandise – including Jacob's Biscuits

Derg Bridge
- Forwardings of turf

Donegal town
- Forwardings of woollen products
- Forwardings of eggs
- Forwarding and receipt of general merchandise
- Connection with CDR road services
- Fowarding and receipt of livestock
- Receipt of fuel oil for railcars and coal for merchants and railway use
- Forwarding and receipt of general merchandise
- Forwarding and receipt of letter mails, parcels and newspapers
- Receipt of coal for local merchants and railway use

Dunkineely – Forwarding and receipt of livestock – there was a cattle and livestock fair here

Killybegs
- Receipt of oil for fishing fleet and railcars
- Receipt of mechanical parts associated with the fishing fleet
- Receipt of agricultural parts and machinery
- Forwarding of fish by rail and road
- Forwarding and receipt of livestock – there was a cattle and livestock fair
- Forwarding of coal from pier and receipt of coal for merchants and locomotive use
- Forwarding and receipt of general merchandise, mails, parcels and newspapers

Ballyshannon
- Cattle and livestock fair
- Receipt of agricultural parts and machinery
- Forwarding and receipt of general merchandise
- Forwarding and receipt of letter mails, parcels and the carriage of newspapers
- Receipt of coal for merchants and railway use
- Receipt of building materials

All stations seemed to handle their fair share of barrels of Guinness, full ones coming in and the empties being swiftly dispatched back! Due to astute management, the CDR was able to hold onto much of this traffic by utilising and expanding its own road fleet following closure of the railway.

There was quite an advanced system of rolling stock control for freight wagons on the CDR and the Appendix to the Working Time Table set out the rules, as follows:

Rolling Stock Control

A return of all wagons on hands, with particulars of those under load to be sent to Manager's Office daily.

Section	Wagons on hands at	Information by	
Letterkenny Line	6.00 pm	6.15 pm train	Following code to be used:
Finn Valley Line	8.00 am	7.50 am train	Goods wagons - 'R'
Glenties Line	7.00 am	7.20 am train	Cattle Wagons - 'C'
Killybegs Line	7.30 am	7.55 am train	Timber Trucks - 'T'
Ballyshannon Line	8.00 am	8.10 am train	Open Wagons - 'F'
NCC	6.00 pm	6.35 pm train	Trans-ship trucks covered - 'BC'
Derry/Strabane	9.00 am	phone	

To avoid unnecessary haulage, terminal and junction stations, as under, will supply empty wagons required for outgoing traffic, stationmasters to requisition accordingly.

To be supplied from

Killybegs line stations	Killybegs
Letterkenny line stations	Letterkenny
Ballyshannon line station	Ballyshannon, Finn Valley, Stranorlar
Glenties line stations	Glenties

MO to be advised if terminal stations cannot supply.
Subject to this, all empty wagons properly labelled, must be worked into Strabane or Derry.
MO will arrange for a supply of cattle wagons, the destination of all such to be phoned and applications for cattle wagons should state the train by which stock is intended to be sent.
When cattle wagons are required at Ballyshannon, latter station must phone Donegal to supply, this request to be complied with, if not available at Donegal, the latter to phone MO.

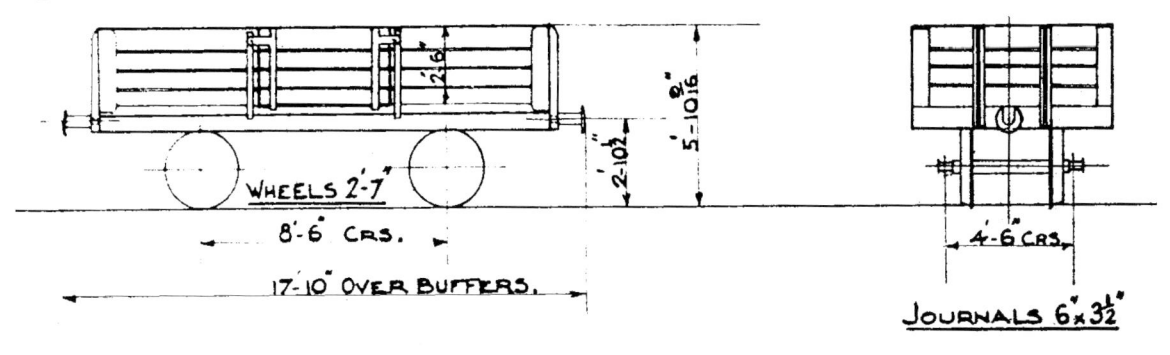

Open Wagons Nos 121–154, 158, 160–168

Both scale: 4 mm to 1 ft

Covered Goods Wagons Nos 46–95, 169–198

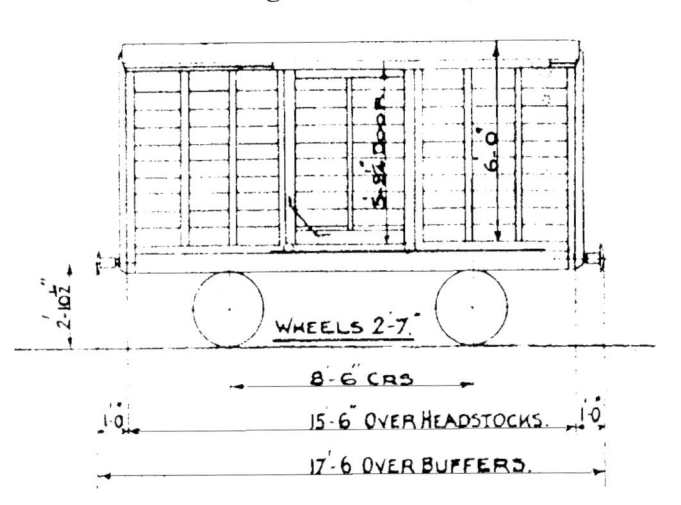

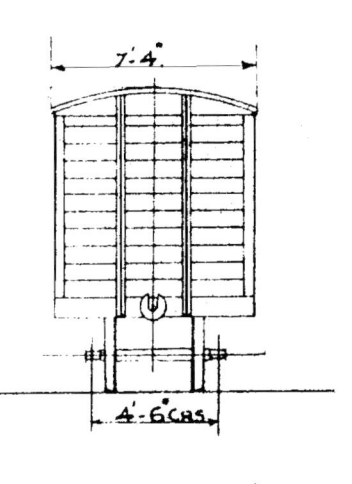

The use of wagons was also to be made in the most efficient way. The rules for this were also set out in the Appendix to the Working Time Table.

Use and Utilisation of Rolling Stock

Following arrangements to be carried out in connection with loading of outwards traffic:

1– When 4 tons or over is received and loaded for a particular station, wagon should be sent direct to that Station, labelled accordingly.

2– Traffic in lots under 4 tons must be dealt with thus:

(a) Glenties line traffic to be loaded up to full carrying capacity of wagon, or may be loaded in a Stranorlar wagon, those mixed for Stranorlar and Glenties line should be labelled for Stranorlar, those fully loaded for the Glenties line, should have labels showing names of stations.

(b) Goods for Killybegs or Ballyshannon lines to be loaded to full carrying capacity of wagon, Ballyshannon and Killybegs line traffic being kept separate. Wagons mixed for Donegal should be labelled to Donegal, wagons not containing traffic for Donegal, but fully loaded for either Killybegs or Ballyshannon lines, should be marshalled and labelled accordingly. The labels showing names of stations.

(c) Small lots for Glenmaquin, Convoy and Raphoe to be loaded in Letterkenny wagons.

(d) Clady, Castlefinn, Liscooly and Killygordon traffic, when tonnage does not justify the use of more than one wagon, should be loaded in a Finn Valley road wagon, not mixed with Stranorlar goods. If it is necessary to use two or more wagons for these stations the traffic should be loaded for a pair of stations in each wagon.

Contents of mixed wagons detached at Stranorlar or Donegal, will be re-sorted (a) Stranorlar (for Glenties line) (b) Donegal (for Ballyshannon and Killybegs lines) and loads concentrated there, enabling surplus wagons to be promptly released and returned to Strabane or Derry. It is not intended that wagons with full loads for Glenties, Ballyshannon or Killybegs lines should be held over at Stranorlar or Donegal, but get a direct connection forward. All concerned should endeavour to stop light loaded wagons on Down Trains, and loads concentrated when possible.

Newspapers were also carried under the following arrangements:

Newspapers

Dublin, Belfast and Cross Channel newspapers may be passed free as charges are raised at sending station and settlement made through I.R.C.H. accounts. The following newspapers are carried by special contract and may also be passed: *Sentinel*, *Journal*, *Standard*, *Strabane Weekly News* and *People's Press*. All returned newspapers must be charged for Messr. Eason's papers and parcels, including subscribers newspapers, to be carried free.

Lastly, parcels were also conveyed.

Stamped Parcels

As a rule these should be put in guards' vans, if it is necessary to load them in ordinary wagons they must be accompanied by a guide way bill to enable them to be picked out. Belfast parcels should be sent via Strabane and GNR Guards and rail-car drivers are supplied with parcel stamps, and at halts, etc., they must affix stamps to the correct value on all parcels handed to them and collect amount from senders or from destination stations, unstamped parcels must not be carried unless specially instructed. A record must be kept of all parcels carried including those transferred from sealed hampers and a note should be made of those in loose order. Sealed parcel hampers must not be up ended but handled flat.

Stranorlar was undoubtedly the 'nerve centre' of the CDR in terms of management, engineering, maintenance and accountancy; Strabane was the 'nerve centre' for the freight business. This was because Strabane was the trans-shipment centre for west, south and east Donegal – like most larger stations it had a five-ton crane and the majority of goods carried by the CDR passed through here. There were two goods trains each day from Strabane to Letterkenny, to Stranorlar in both directions and then further west from Stranorlar to Killybegs. The type of goods being carried were, as illustrated by the lists above, extremely varied. On the inwards side, goods were for shops, farmers and builders merchants, consumables ranging from biscuits to beer. (Beer being an important commodity, it was not uncommon to have a wagon full of barrels of Guinness.) Bread hampers were carried, as were insulated boxes of ice cream from the big ice cream works in Dublin at Inchicore: these would be moved by railcar as they were perishable and thus needed to be delivered with greater speed.

The railcars would carry the majority of mails and newspapers, the latter ranging up to 17 titles under contract on a daily or weekly basis. Latterly there were small containers carrying biscuits from the Jacob's works in Dublin and open wagons would be used to carry sand, gravel and timber. There were three main types of wagon on the CDR: the open wagon, which could be described as a flat wagon; the cattle-type wagon which had drop doors for ventilation and to help with cleaning; and finally the closed covered goods wagons.

On the export side, the main freight was turf, Donegal being a turf-bearing county and Glenties having a turf-production works. Trains of turf would move to Strabane for eventual use in Dublin and the other main cities. In the trans-ship shed at Strabane, a group of 40 men, known as the 'Tonnage Gang', were employed to shovel turf from narrow to standard gauge. They were paid on a tonnage rate and were involved in transferring turf and bog ore, the latter used for smelting. Wool for export was a big trans-shipment item, Donegal also being a sheep-rearing county. The wool was brought by large wool merchants – the likes of Willie Mulraney in Donegal town and Mick Marley in Cloghan – baled and trans-shipped onto the GNR trains at Strabane, not only for Ireland but for England. Potatoes were also a large export item. They grew easily in Donegal, and were less affected by the Great Famine of 1845–49 than the rest of the country, possibly because Donegal is closer to the sea. Seed potatoes were grown in Donegal and sent to Cyprus via Derry – these being inspected by the Éire Department of Agriculture authorities in Derry to ensure that only the finest went out.

Livestock was a considerable export – many cattle trains ran to Derry for onward shipment to England and Scotland, while sheep were also carried, mainly from farm to market or fairs. There was a very big sheep fair held annually in Brockagh near Cloghan on the Glenties line, and there was another near Letterkenny. Horses, asses or mules also travelled to and from other fairs. Pigs were also carried. It was once reported that a farmer had arrived at a small wayside station without having ordered his wagon. The guard on the train took the pig into his van and travelled with it to its destination – much to his disgust, but illustrating the commitment to the customer!

Killybegs is Ireland's biggest fishing town and produced large supplies of the product. The fish would often be iced and boxed in Killybegs and then sent out on the 07.20 railcar in the morning in the red wagon. It would be iced again at Strabane, a special crew from the trans-ship shed being allocated this task. Fish was also carried by CDR road services so as to reach the Dublin fish market as soon as possible. This was a seven-day-a-week, 365-days-a-year operation, the lorries bringing back the empty fish crates.

Coal was an important incoming item from Derry and from Killybegs. It was used for locomotive fuel and various merchants along the line. The coal from Killybegs was taken in the main to Ballyshannon and the town's principal coal merchant, Morgan. It also was shipped to Convoy woollen mills on the Letterkenny road.

The other main export traffic was empty beer bottles, crates, hogs heads, and firkins, as Guinness and beer was a large import! These would all go back to the Guinness factory in Dublin.

Customs clearance was a major impediment to the passage of goods trains – traffic into Éire being handled at Castlefinn or Lifford, and that into the North at Strabane. The operation of special goods trains were common – notification in advance was by circular or telephone. 'Specials' would be employed when unusually large loads of goods arrived at Strabane on the GN, but it was easy enough to put together a goods train to cope with this.

The tonnages allowed behind one locomotive on the lines varied, depending on the gradients:

Strabane–Derry:	230 tons
Strabane–Letterkenny:	165–170 tons – hence it took two or three services a day as traffic was heavy
Strabane–Stranorlar:	450 tons (reflecting the flat nature of the old Finn Valley road)
Strabane–Glenties:	205–180 tons
Stranorlar–Donegal:	185 tons
Donegal–Ballyshannon:	185–205 tons
Donegal–Killybegs:	150–160 tons

No 5 *Drumboe* stands alongside some tanker and open wagons at Strabane in June 1953. The railcar and locomotive running shed is to the rear and the trans-shipment shed is over to the right. To the right, wagon No 157 stands in a line. She was built in 1900 by Oldbury and is seen carrying a Shell Oil tank, as is the wagon behind her. These tanks sat in a type of cradle and could be lifted in and out by using lifting hoists on the side of the tank.

JM Jarvis/ColourRail

No 5 *Drumboe* is seen marshalling wagons at Strabane for a freight service to Stranorlar on 2 August 1958. The shunter Tobias McLaughlin, sometimes known as Jimmy, climbs off the locomotive steps. Strabane was the hub of CDR freight services and the interchange with the Great Northern can be seen with the trans-shipment shed in the background. GN wagons are also seen on the right.

ES Russell/ColourRail

No 5 *Drumboe* continues her shunting on 2 August 1958 to make up a longer train. The man walking beside the train is Jimmy 'Shunty' Doherty and Francie McMenamin is on the footplate.
ES Russell/ColourRail

Tractor No 11 *Phoenix* moves an open wagon and a red wagon around Strabane station on 2 August 1958. *Phoenix* was central to the shunting operations at Strabane, moving wagons detached from railcars or moving trains to and from Lifford or Castlefinn for customs clearance.
ES Russell/ColourRail

No 5 *Drumboe* has completed the marshalling of its freight for Stranorlar at Strabane on 2 August 1958. As all CDRJC freights were fully fitted, the guard's accommodation was in a passenger van, which has now been added.
ES Russell/ColourRail

A year earlier, on 8 June 1957, 'Baltic' tank No 11 *Erne* has a short freight (possibly agricultural machinery) for Letterkenny at Strabane. She also has in tow a covered wagon and the passenger van for the guard.
K Cooper/ColourRail

No 2 *Blanche* is seen at Letterkenny, shunting wagons off a freight she has brought in from Strabane. Wagon 173 was a covered wagon built in a batch (numbers 169–198) by the Metropolitan Carriage and Wagon works in 1905. Next to it is open wagon No 297, built by Hurst Nelson in 1909 in the batch numbered 295–304. It appears to be carrying some sort of tank – probably for agricultural purposes. The 'X' on the side means that it has no train brakes, but is through piped.

The General Appendix to the working Time Table mentions the handling of tanks as follows :

Oil Tank Wagons and Oil Containers

Oil tank wagons owned by Shell and Anglo Companies, vacuum fitted, may be worked on any train but marshalled on rear if possible; great care should be taken at Strabane when transferring the oil containers by crane.

ColourRail

No 1 *Alice* is seen at Letterkenny on 19 May 1956, also shunting and preparing a freight to return to Strabane. The shunter is Jimmy Murray. Wagon No 51 can be seen to the right of the locomotive. No 51 was built in 1893 in a large batch, Nos 46–95. Oatfield's sweet factory is seen in the background.

ES Russell/ColourRail

101

No 4 *Meenglas* has arrived with a freight at Castlefinn on 22 June 1959. The train is undergoing a customs check and the coach has been included for enthusiasts. Wagon No 255 of 1908 vintage, the first of a batch numbered 255–284, built by Hurst Nelson, is being unloaded on the right. At Castlefinn, the name was spelt with one 'N' on the right-hand platform in this photograph but with two 'N's on the other!
ColourRail

On 22 May 1956, No 11 *Erne* arrives at Castlefinn with a freight. The customs check could be an examination of one wagon, or to ensure that the paper work was correct for what was on the train. If it was not, the goods were taken off and put in a bond store. The signal in the foreground is a magnificent example of a CDR signal, in excellent condition.
ES Russell/ColourRail

This picture captures the scene as crates are picked up for the local pub at Castlefinn on 22 May 1956. Virtually everything came in by rail! The man in the red jersey, surname Tinney, was one of the family that owned the pub.

ES Russell/ColourRail

No 4 *Meenglas* is seen at Castlefinn on 18 May 1959 waiting for customs inspection to be completed. In the train is a bogie open wagon, most likely converted from a coach chassis. The trestle table for passenger customs inspections can be seen in the shed, used on wet days, otherwise the procedure was carried out in the open. The other building to the right is the customs officers room for uniformed men. On the other side were the customs clearance clerk, stationmaster's office and stationmaster's clerk. The two porter signalmen, in between trains, would help in the bond or goods store.

C Gammell/ColourRail

No 11 *Erne* is seen on a Stranorlar to Strabane freight at Killygordon. That smoke makes it look as if the washing may have to be re-done! The stationmaster here, Willie MacIntyre, had a very large family which probably explains the amount of washing. He was to finish his career at Raphoe. Killygordon had sidings and the end of one wagon can just be seen in here.

P Whitehouse/ColourRail

No 2 *Blanche* is at Stranorlar East on 13 September 1957, shunting wagons. Danny Montieth, the shunter/guard, is on the footplate with Francie McMenamin to the right. Behind the train is the goods store and to the rear of that is the Curran residence. To the right is the loading dock and it looks as though some sort of farm machinery has been delivered and is awaiting collection. To the rear is a passenger van awaiting its next turn of duty. The locomotive is in immaculate condition.

C Hogg/ColourRail

A lengthy, but typical CDR goods train hauled by an unidentified Class 5 locomotive gets away from Letterkenny for Lifford and Strabane. There are container wagons in the middle of the train which may be carrying machinery of some kind or returning empty.

DWK Jones/ColourRail

No 2 *Blanche* makes a fine sight as she leaves Donegal town for Stranorlar. This train has been seen earlier in the book at Donegal (page 35), and has four carriages followed by oil tankers and goods wagons. These carriages are being worked back empty and have been included in the freight train.

P Whitehouse/ColourRail

Covered Goods Wagons Nos 255–284

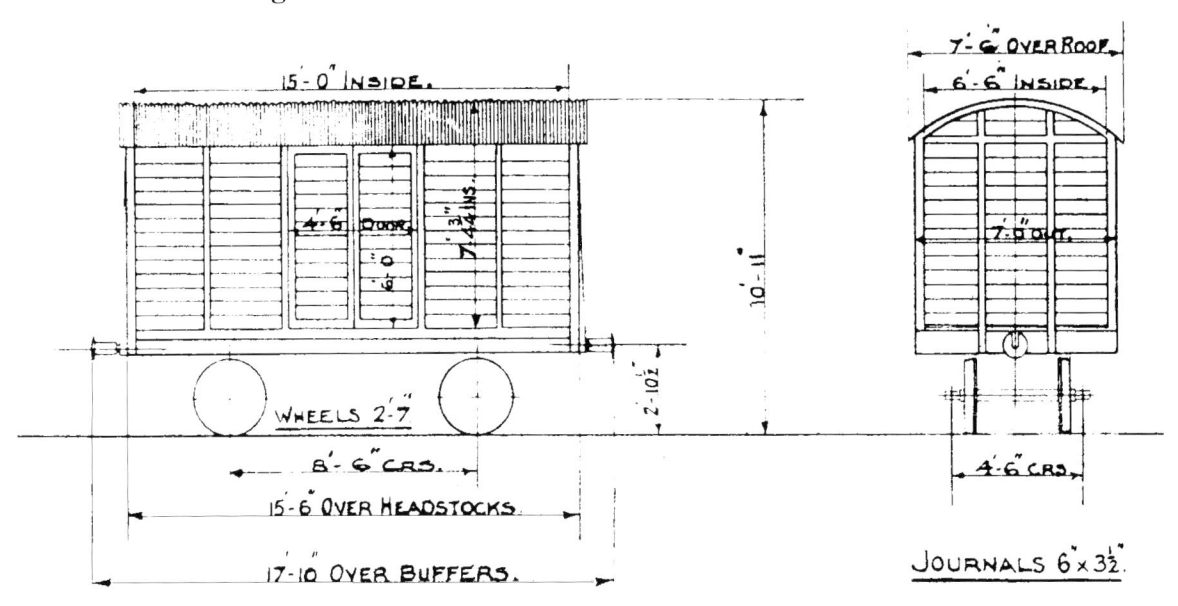

Bogie Wagon No 159

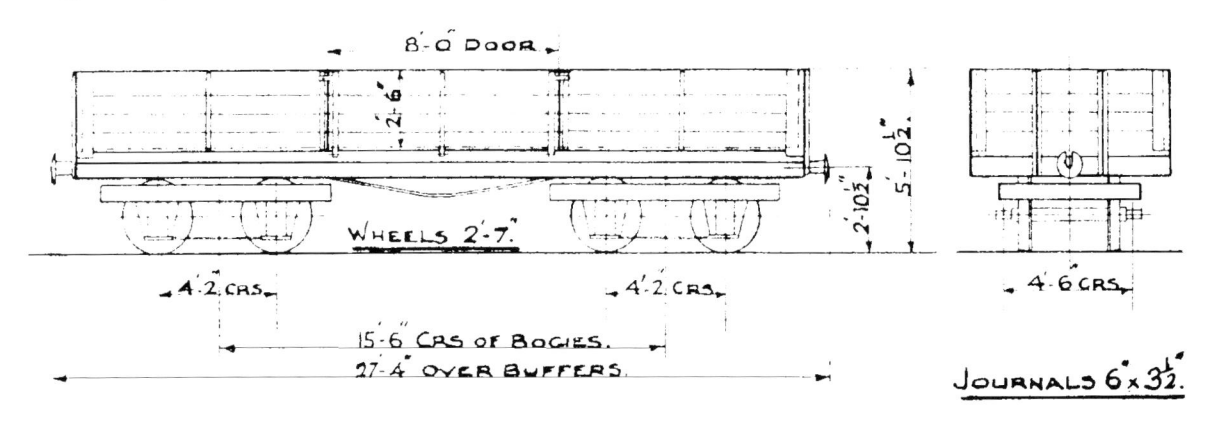

Open wagons Nos 41, 42, 45, 101–117, 156, 234–238, 249–250, 295–304, 305, 307–08, 309, 311

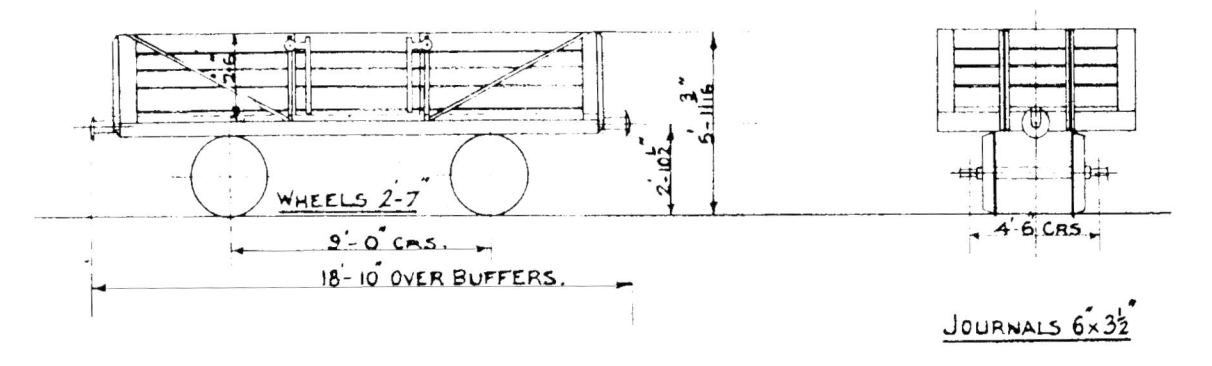

All scale: 4 mm to 1 ft

THE BUS REPLACEMENTS

From 1 January 1960, the CDR switched to being a total road operation, the bus services running to approximately the same timetable as the trains. To meet demand for these extra services, the CDR purchased six used Leyland 'Tiger Cubs' to add to their fleet and to return six on hire to CIÉ. They were excellent vehicles, but really too light for the heavy Donegal Hills and the indifferent roads.

These buses had number plates from ORR 330 onwards. Five of the six are viewed here, with one is missing, being in service. All seven buses here are in CDR livery.

J Curran

Michael Boyle stands next to Leyland 'Tiger Cub' ORR 332 at Stranorlar. Note the excellent condition of the vehicle. Michael joined the CDR in the late 1940s as the man in charge at Lough Eske. After closure he became a bus conductor on CDR routes and became Road Service Inspector at Donegal, responsible for all services in the area. He retired in 1990 and died in August 1999. This career demonstrates the level of commitment and service from CDR employees to the general public, whether for passenger or freight services and whether by rail or road.

J Curran

Co. Donegal Railways Joint Committee
ROAD PASSENGER SERVICES

```
+++++++++++++++++++++++++++
+     WHITSUNTIDE - 1966.   +
+++++++++++++++++++++++++++
```

The following arrangements will apply:-

FRIDAY, 27th MAY	–	Normal Services.
SATURDAY, 28th MAY.	–	Normal Services.
SUNDAY, 29th MAY.	–	No Services.
WHIT MONDAY, 30th MAY.	–	Full Service as under:-

STRABANE-DONEGAL-KILLYBEGS ROUTE.

		a.m.	a.m.	p.m.	p.m.		
STRABANE	dep.	7.40	11.30	3.25	6.25	...	...
Ballybofey	arr.	8.19	12.10	4.05	7.00	...	...
"	dep.	8.20	12.20	4.40	...	...	...
Donegal	arr.	8.55	12.55	5.15	...	...	...
"	dep.	9.00	...	6.15	...	...	...
KILLYBEGS	arr.	10.00	...	7.15	...	...	...

		a.m.	a.m.	p.m.	p.m.	p.m.	p.m.
KILLYBEGS	dep.	...	9.40	1.00	...	...	...
Donegal	arr.	...	10.40	2.00	...	...	...
"	dep.	...	11.00	2.05	...	...	6.05
Ballybofey	arr.	...	11.35	2.40	...	...	6.40
"	dep.	9.45	...	2.45	4.05	5.45	...
STRABANE	arr.	10.20	...	3.20	4.45	6.25	...

STRABANE-RAPHOE-LETTERKENNY ROUTE.

		a.m.	p.m.	p.m.			
STRABANE	dep.	8.45	2.10	5.10	...	...	...
Raphoe	"	9.05	2.32	5.30	...	...	...
LETTERKENNY	arr.	9.40	3.05	6.05	...	...	...

		a.m.	p.m.	p.m.			
LETTERKENNY	dep.	11.35	3.50	6.10	...	...	...
Raphoe	"	12.08	4.23	6.44	...	...	...
STRABANE	arr.	12.30	4.45	7.05	...	...	...

SLIGO-BALLYBOFEY-DERRY ROUTE
BALLYBOFEY-GLENTIES-PORTNOO "
BALLYBOFEY-LETTERKENNY "
DONEGAL-PORTNOO "
KILLYBEGS-MALINMORE "
ROSSNOWLAGH-BALLYSHANNON "
GLENTIES-DUNGLOE "

For details of services on these routes, please refer to notices issued by Coras Iompair Eireann.

STRANORLAR,
16th MAY, 1966.

B.L. CURRAN.
MANAGER & SECRETARY.